OMNIBUS

TREVOR WYE

PRACTICE BOOKS for the *flute*

NOVELLO

A PREFACE TO BE READ

TO THE STUDENT

These books are about practising; how to extract the most from it, how to be more efficient at it and how to isolate and overcome some of the difficulties of the flute. They are by no means intended to be definitive. They were written to help you achieve good results with many of the flute problems, in the shortest time. If the exercises are played properly, it will shorten the time spent on the building blocks of flute playing, and so allow more time for music making.

These points about practising in general, are important:
(a) Practise the flute only because you want to; if you don't want to – don't! It is almost useless to spend your allocated practice time wishing that you weren't practising.
(b) Having decided to practise, make it difficult. Like a pest inspector, examine every corner of your tone and technique for flaws and practise to remove them. Only by this method will you improve quickly. After glancing through these books, you will see that many of the exercises are simply a way of looking at the same problem from different angles. You will not find it difficult to invent new ways.
(c) Try always to practise what you can't play. Don't indulge in too much self-flattery by playing through what you can already do well.
(d) As many of the exercises are taxing, be sure your posture and hand positions are correct. It is important to consult a good teacher on these points – see page 9 in Practice Book 6 (Advanced Practice).

GUARANTEE

Possession of these books is no guarantee that you will improve on the flute; there is no magic in the printed paper. But, if you have the desire to play well and put in some reasonable practice, you cannot fail to improve. It is simply a question of *time, patience* and *intelligent work*. This series of books is designed to avoid unnecessary practice. It is concentrated stuff. *Provided* that you follow the instructions carefully, you should make more than twice the improvement in half the time! *That is the guarantee.*

TO THE TEACHER

This series of basic exercise books is for players of all ages who have been learning from about a year up to and including students at music colleges and universities. There are some recommended speeds, but these should be chosen to accommodate the ability of the player. Some exercises are more difficult than others: take what you feel your students need.

Trevor Wye

TREVOR WYE

OMNIBUS EDITION BOOKS 1-5

PRACTICE BOOKS for the *flute*

VOLUME 1

Tone

For Micky

CONTENTS

TONE EXERCISES – GENERAL This book is not concerned with any particular school of playing, national style, or with any particular concept of sound production. A good teacher should be your guide. The exercises should be played with your eyes shut; perceptive hearing is thereby enhanced.

Listen carefully *all* the time.
Try not to be distracted by events around you.
If your tone is rudimentary it would be better to start with the low register and build on that.

I have never forgotten the preface to Marcel Moyse' admirable *De la Sonorité*, in which he says, 'It is a question of *time*, *patience* and *intelligent work*'.

POSSESSION OF THIS BOOK IS NOT ENOUGH.

TONE

When tone is discussed, the word tone is used as a collective noun for a number of desirable qualities, any or each of which contribute a significant part of the overall 'tone'.

For example:
(a) colour
(b) size
(c) projection
(d) intensity
(e) vibrato
(f) purity

If the tone contains desirable quantities of any or all of these ingredients, then it is said to be beautiful. A player's tone is only as good as its weakest aspect. It must be seen that it is impossible to practise any one of these qualities without incorporating others.
Presuming that anyone who takes up a flute and blows it *desires* to produce a pleasant tone, it is difficult *not* to get a sound which, to most ears at least, gives pleasure. The flute head is *made* to give certain tonal qualities which most people would call beautiful.
Therefore, if a student plays long, slow notes to give him opportunity to examine his tone in close detail, then, provided he can *hear* the undesirable aspects of his tone, his self-correcting mechanism will ensure that it improves. Long notes really can't fail to improve your tone!
Nevertheless, long slow notes played without care and thought will not achieve any *real* result quickly. The object of this book is to present a series of steps in tone building, which, if played with intelligence and patience, will achieve the desired result in the shortest time.

HARMONICS

Harmonics, or overtones are the ingredients in sound which give the basic or 'fundamental' tone its colour and character. For the young player, the low and high registers are both difficult but let it be understood that unless the low register tone contains overtones or some richness and colour, the middle and high registers will be the more difficult. Some practice first on overtones will be advantageous.

Ex. 1: Learn to place the notes exactly without them splitting. This is very beneficial.

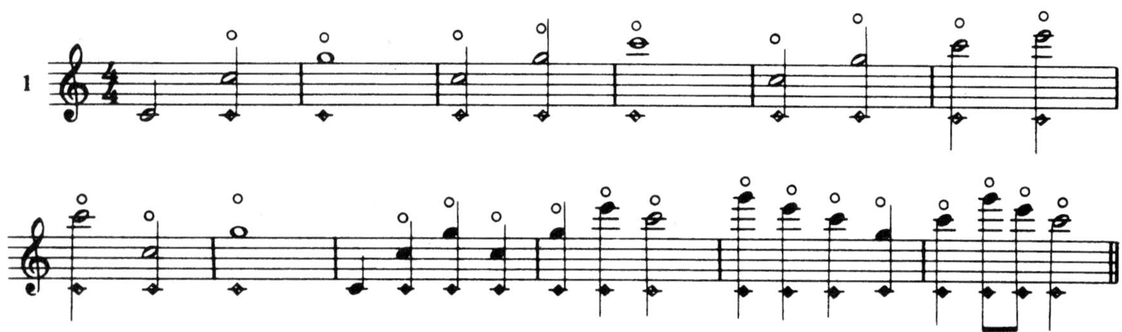

Then try some bugle calls.

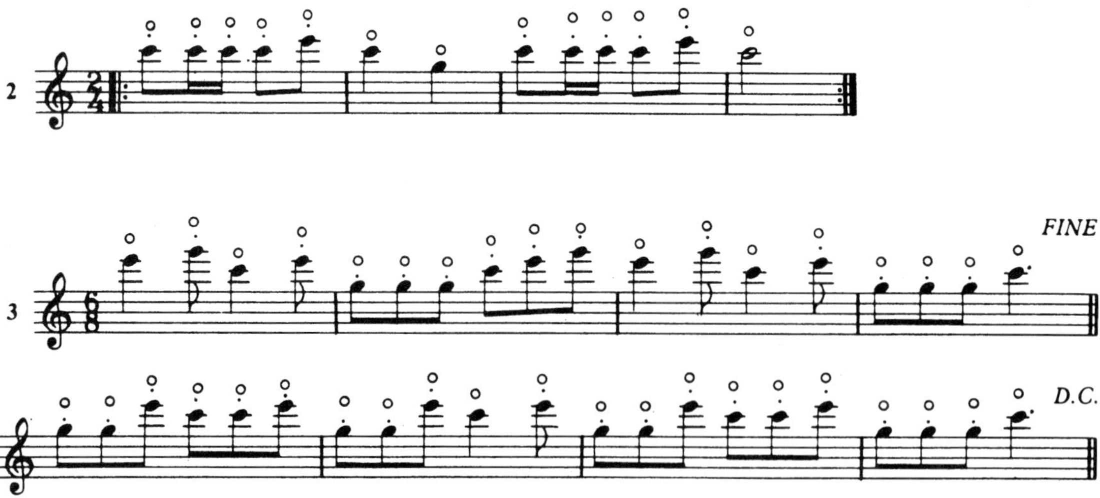

Repeat the three exercises above, fingering (a) low C sharp (b) low D natural (c) low E flat. Notice the increase in air speed required for the higher overtones

THE LOW REGISTER

Whether you begin here or on the later exercises depends on your needs and the advice of your teacher. Assuming that you wish to start by putting the roots of your future tone work firmly in the ground, practise the lower register. But first, you must practise B natural, the easiest note on the flute. It's easy because (a) the shorter the tube the easier the notes are to play and (b) both finger and thumb are holding the flute firmly, a security not so readily available for the two notes above B natural. Play this note – B natural – for as long as it takes to play the best, brightest, most beautiful, rich B natural you've ever played in your life. It *may* take 10-15 minutes. Fine! Unless you have a train to catch, you will achieve more by practising this note than by trying to cover pages of exercises.

Don't play a series of short Bs. Play each B natural for as long as your breath lasts.

When the B natural is really good, commence Exercise 1. Each pair of notes should use up nearly all your air supply; therefore, play them very slowly. Try to ensure that each pair of notes has the *same* quality. Take care not to turn the flute *in* when descending. If the second note happens to sound *better* than the first note, then play each pair backwards.

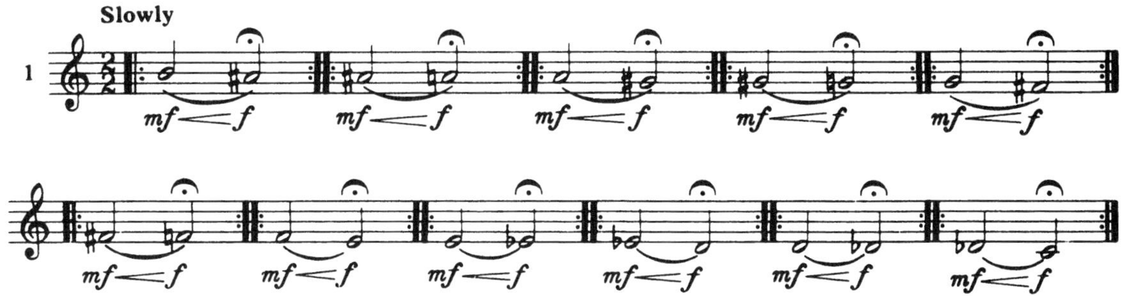

Don't force the tone in the last three bars; it is more difficult to get a good tone here. These last bars may need to be repeated many times.

On your first few days, exercise 1 may well take twenty minutes. Don't worry. There are no prizes for playing the fastest. After several days of practice it is a common complaint that the tone has become worse. This is because your perception of sound is now more acute. Probably your tone *has* improved but having played notes long enough to actually *hear* what is wrong, you are perhaps more aware of your tonal deficiencies.

Now add Exercises 2, 3 and 4 to your practice of No. 1. Remember to repeat each bar just as often as necessary. Not just because it's printed but because you need it!

It is a question of *time*, *patience* and *intelligent work*!

Always start and end your tone practice with a good B natural. It is your reference tone.

*As mentioned before, these last few notes get progressively more difficult. This is because the effective flute tube whilst getting longer does not become wider in bore. If it did, the lower notes would be somewhat easier to play though they would also have a different quality. The tone of the second and third octaves would also be impaired.

You can now add these next three exercises to your repertoire of long notes. Small adjustments are made to the lips when descending. Take care not to sound like a paper bag full of wasps on your low notes; avoid turning the flute inwards on the lip when descending. Remember to practise the B natural first.

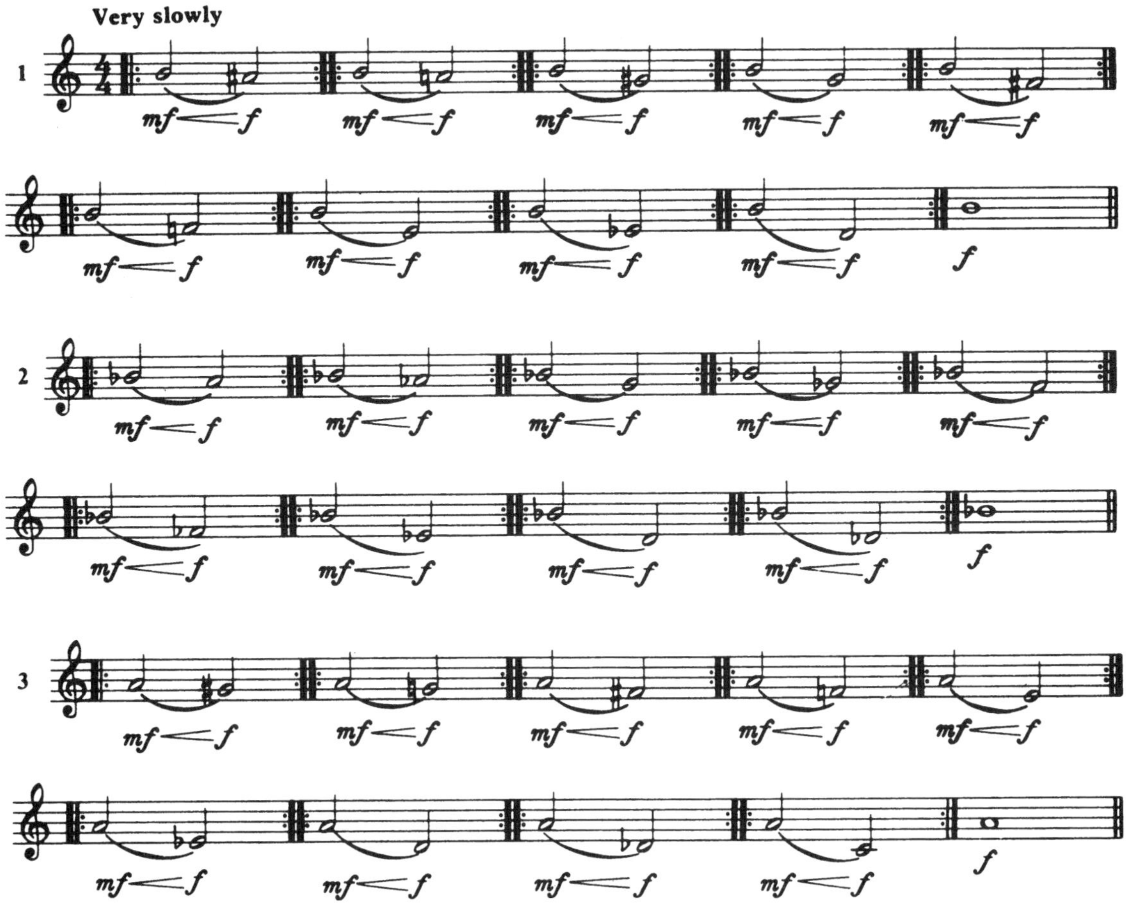

As you become more advanced, here are three more low-register exercises to practise based on:
1) 'The Aquarium' variation from *Carnival of the Animals* by Saint-Saens,
2) a theme from the *Introduction and Allegro* by Ravel, for septet and
3) *Prélude à l'après-midi d'un faune* by Debussy.

1) *The Aquarium* This needs a hollow, 'pure' tone which will be called a 'yellow' tone.* Think of deep, dark green water and silent fish swimming gracefully about. Don't forget to practise B natural first followed by C in preparation for this exercise. See also the section 'The Chord of Nature'—Practice Book IV—INTONATION.

*A further explanation of tone colours appears in PROPER FLUTE PLAYING, pp. 17-19 (Novello) where these exercises are more fully discussed, and in Practice Book VI – ADVANCED PRACTICE, p.6.

★ (see contents)

2) Ravel[§] The Ravel theme needs a somewhat darker, richer tone colour, which we will call 'purple'.

3) Debussy's *Prélude à l'après-midi d'un faune.*

Here are four low-register exercises based on this well-known theme. Use this exercise to practise a colour somewhere between 'yellow' and 'purple'.

§*Introduction and Allegro for Septet.* Editions Durand, Paris/United Music Publishers Ltd. By permission.

PREPARATION
mf
mf
Slowly
a)
PREPARATION
f
f
Slowly
b)
(V)
PREPARATION
Slowly
c)
3

PREPARATION
Slowly
d)
(V)
mf
f
FINAL EXERCISE
Slowly
a)
b)
c)
d)

THE MIDDLE REGISTER – I

First, find a good left hand low-register note. It must be your *best* note.

When the note of your choice sounds beautiful, slur up an octave without becoming tense. Don't raise the air stream too high when ascending or the upper note will sound *thin*. Experiment keeping the air stream as low as is practicable in the upper octave and without covering more of the blow-hole. If your upper octave note is not B, slowly ascend to B and practise it for a few moments to make it as bright and as beautiful as possible.

You are going to spread the sound of the B natural downwards into the low register. Therefore, before infecting the low notes, make quite certain that the B natural is a veritable Archangel Gabriel of a B natural before attempting to make the A sharp sound just as good.

As in earlier exercises, play each pair of notes for nearly as long as your breath lasts. Only proceed if the previous pair of notes have been repeated many times to ensure *evenness of quality*. Endeavour also to make the second note even *better* than the first. If this happens at any point, reverse the exercise and work back to B natural which should be even better by this time.

As far as G, all should go well though from G natural to E natural is the first problem patch. Don't force the notes. If these notes sound clear, then proceed. However, for most people, this area from G natural down to E natural has its problems. This is due, once again, to the tube width in relation to its length. This narrowing 'tightens' the notes and causes them sometimes to split. It is during these exercises that you can find out how far you can push a note before it splits. Evenness of tone is what you must strive for.

On descending, if the lower note sounds *better* than the upper one, then reverse the exercise to make the 'reference note' a better reference note!

When some improvement has been made, go back to B natural.

When you reach E flat, there is often a distinct difference in quality. This is the second problem area. Proceed as before, improving the E flat from both the E natural and the D natural.

Ensure that the first finger left hand is raised for E flat and D.*
Raising the first finger for E flat clears this note of its stuffiness. If this area still presents great difficulty, try proceeding by sequential steps.

After some days of practice, add Exercise 4 to your daily session. It joins two bars of Exercise 1 together. The tone quality should be the same. Remember to practise the B natural first.

When some success has been gained, add the following two exercises to your repertoire:

**N.B.* *Exercises for this problem can be found in the companion volumes to this book: VOL. II – TECHNIQUE and VOL. III – ARTICULATION.*

The last bar – above – is there to remind you of problem No. 3: the area around C sharp which is dealt with in the next section. As you descend, the C sharp is the outstandingly empty note. With a different fingering, let us make a *resonant* note out of C sharp, one which, with the *correct* fingering, can be imitated. Whilst descending from D to C sharp, finger C sharp as for *low* C sharp. You must, of course, overblow it. It is full of overtones but it gives one something to grip on. Now try to obtain that same resonance, and *tuning*, with all the fingers off as in the usual fingering. On many flutes, C sharp sounds a little better with the second and third fingers down of the right hand. Try this too, if it helps.

Notice that the C natural sounds better than the C sharp. Check the tuning of both with the overtones* of low C and low C sharp.

**Additional exercises to check the tuning and tone of C and C sharp can be found in the section 'Pitch Control' – III. It is useless to practise obtaining C and C sharp with a good tone if the intonation is defective. Get rid of your acne before applying make-up!*

Starting with low B, work at the C sharp from this end of the compass.

When some success has been gained, try from both ends.

Then from B natural work your way back up again to the upper B natural. Remember that each phrase is played *very slowly*.

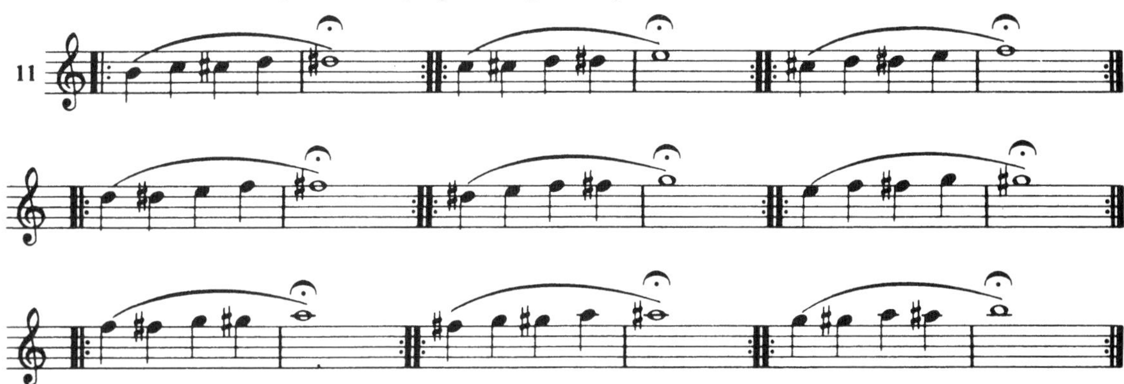

In Exercise 10, you will try to obtain evenness from middle B natural down to low C natural. Start off with pairs of notes as in Exercise 1. Then as progress is made, use Exercises 4, 5, 6 and 10 as your pattern.

You should by now be some way on towards solving the problems of the middle register. Your tone will not improve evenly throughout the range of notes so far studied, though you should now be equipped with enough ideas on how to tackle the difficult areas. It is a question of__________, ____________and___________ ________!

THE MIDDLE REGISTER – II

When both lower and middle registers have been practised for some months, you may find there is still a rather different colour between the lower and middle registers. This exercise will help iron out major differences. Whatever colour you start on, *keep that colour into the middle register.* Practise this exercise first with the 'yellow' aquarium colour, and after, with the Ravel colour, 'purple' (see also PROPER FLUTE PLAYING, p.19).

12 **Slowly** ★

mf — f

★At this point you will use the colour of the note to help penetrate the leap into the upper note.

PREPARATION FOR

THE HIGH REGISTER

These exercises will help to iron out any change in colour from the middle register to the high register.
They will also help you to 'penetrate' the upper notes – as in the previous section.
Don't raise the air stream too much or your tone will become thin and squeaky.
Endeavour to make the high register sound *noble.*
Top E natural and F sharp are often problem notes. See the section on *Gnomes.*
Using colours in the top register is more difficult, but practise to obtain even a small difference between 'yellow' and 'purple'.

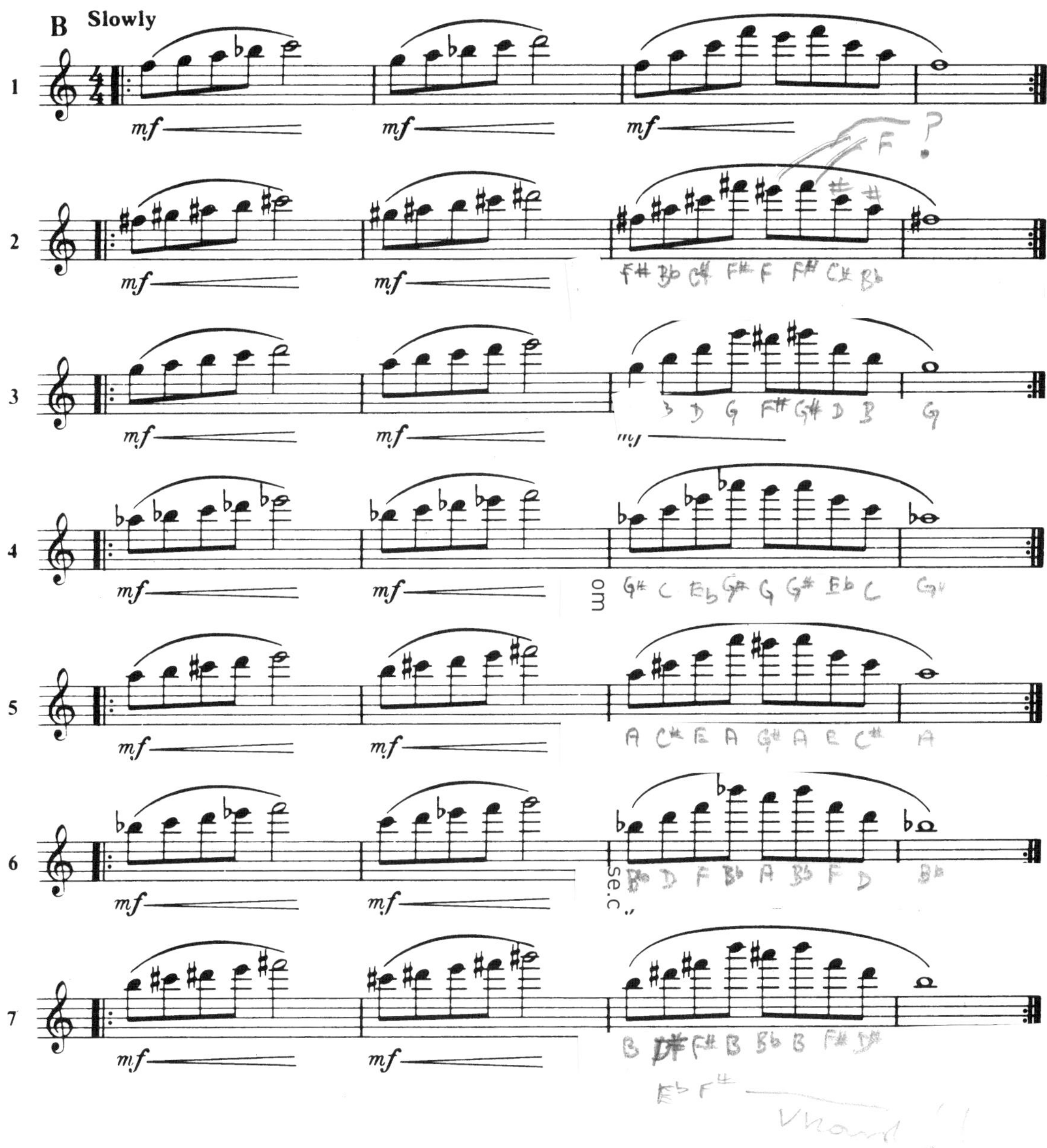

THE HIGH REGISTER

Perhaps these first two octaves have been difficult but the high register is certainly the *most* difficult in which to obtain a good sonority, colour, and depth of tone.
Be sure, before attempting these exhausting exercises, to thoroughly cover the ground in the first two octaves*.
It is better not to practise the high register in the same practice session as the middle and lower registers. Try to do it later in the day.

Remember: it is a question of______, __________and____________________ ______!
You also need understanding neighbours!

**See also the next section on* Gnomes.

Exercise 1: use the same method of working as for the lower and middle registers. Avoid becoming tense as you ascend.

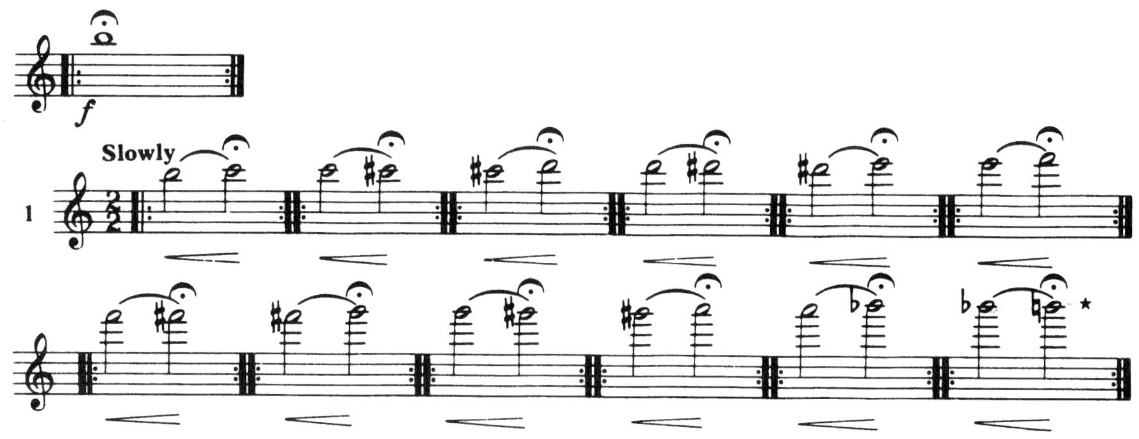

No D sharp key for top B natural

If you wish, go on to high C, C sharp and D, but only if you have the embouchure strength to do this without becoming rigid and tense.

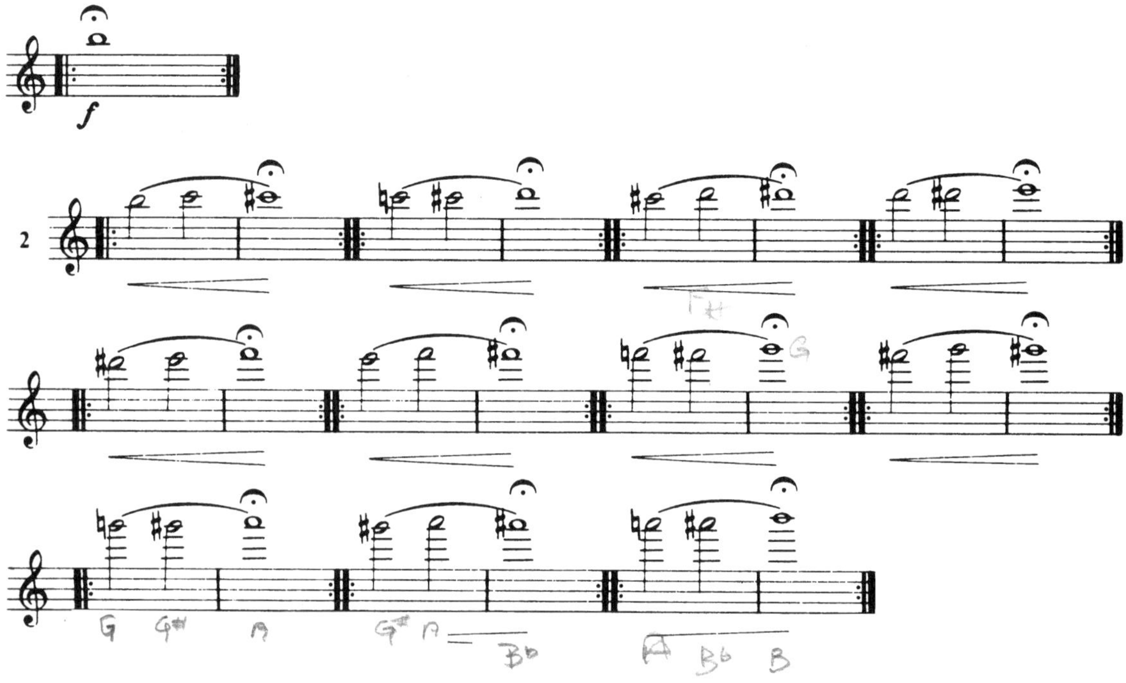

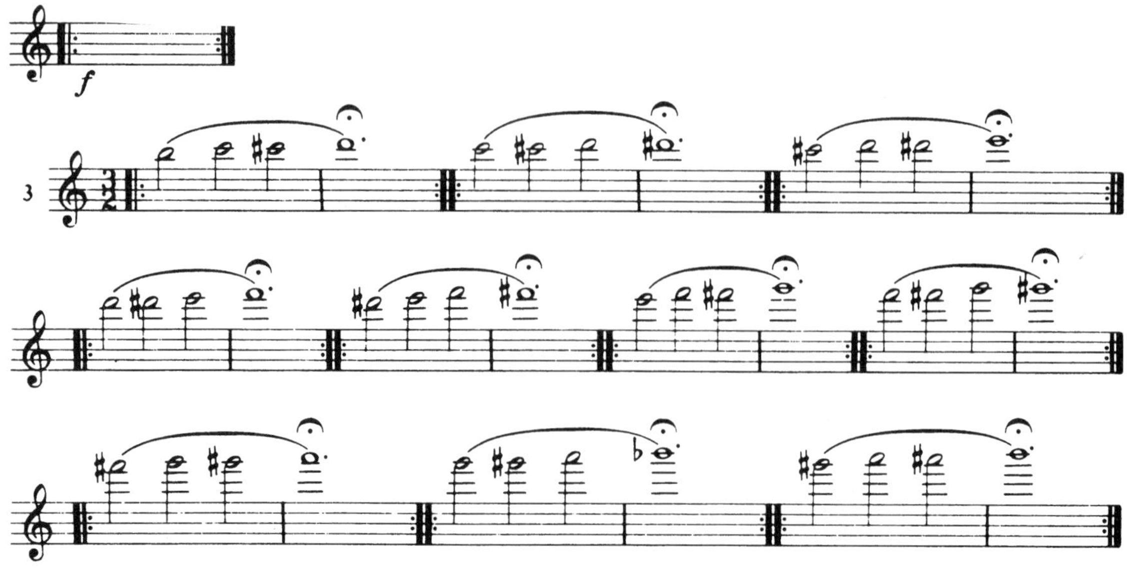

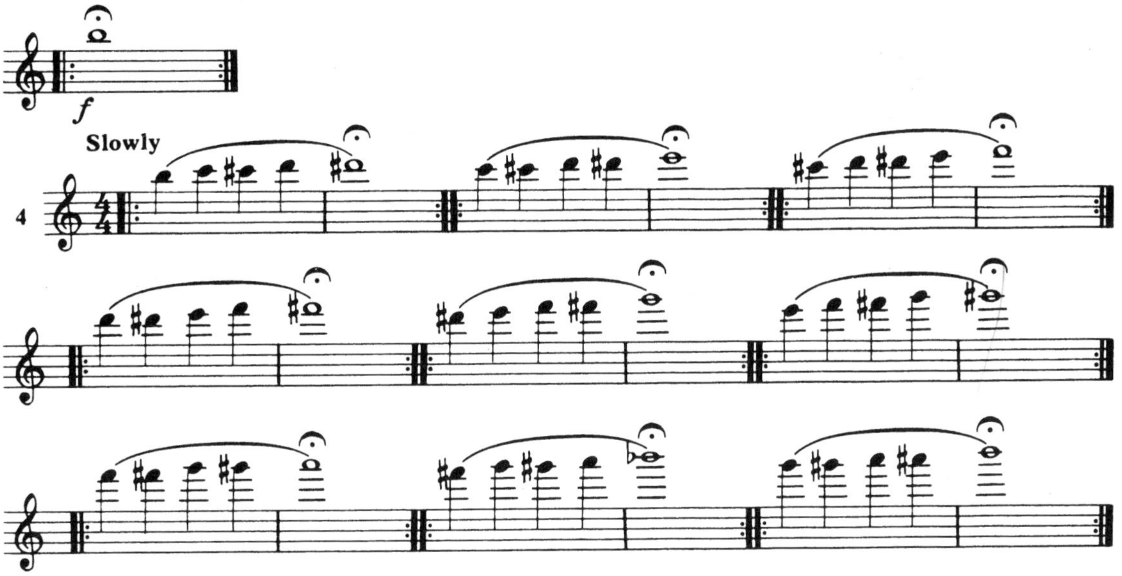

f

Slowly

4

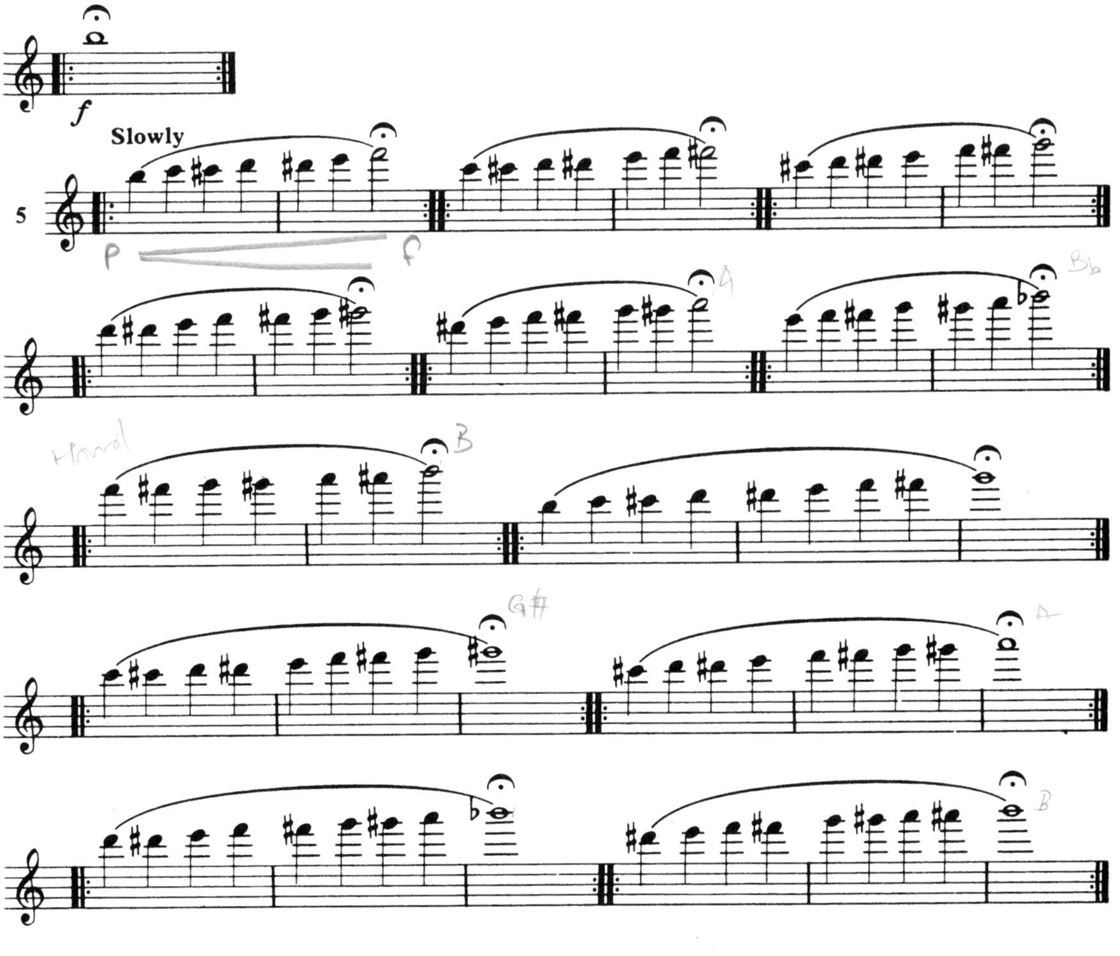

Slowly

5

As your work progresses and your lips become stronger, *change the nuances* so as to practise these exercises both *piano* and *forte*.

GNOMES – E natural and F sharp

You may have noticed that top E natural and F sharp are rather sharp. They are also more difficult (without a split E mechanism) than the surrounding notes. There is a mechanical reason for this; if you finger the low register chromatically from low E flat up to B flat, and without blowing, directly compare the fingering with that of the high register, you will see that, apart from E natural and F sharp, there is, in general, one hole open for the comparable upper note. That is, *except* for E natural and F sharp.
Without a split E mechanism, these two notes have *two* holes uncovered with the *comparable* low-register note. If one hole could be closed – as on a split E mechanism flute – top E natural would be easier. A mechanism *has* been invented to close one of the two holes for top F sharp thereby making that easier too. It is called a split F sharp mechanism and is very complex and expensive. It is just another mechanical part which can all too easily go wrong.
With thoughtful practice, I am convinced that neither of these two 'aids' are necessary. With a split E mechanism, indeed the F sharp seems to be more difficult for *psychological* reasons!
Play the scale of G:

The air speed increases when ascending this scale. If difficulty or uncertainty is experienced in obtaining E natural or F sharp then the *air speed* is insufficient to obtain it given that the direction of the air is right. With young players this is a common problem. If, in ascending the scale *piano*, the E natural or F sharp do not sound, then *the notes building up to E natural and F sharp – G, A, B, C and D are the ones to practise.*
If the air speed is not enough to give security to E natural and F sharp then the air speed is probably insufficient to play the *preceding* notes *with proper intensity of sound.*

THINK ABOUT THIS BEFORE PROCEEDING.
In Exercise 1 use more air speed than appears to be necessary to obtain the notes in the first two phrases. No difficulty should then be experienced in bars 6 and 10.

Earlier we discovered that E natural and F sharp are both rather sharp notes. Compare the pitch of them with the harmonics of low C and D.

Of course, E natural and F sharp are here being played as fifth harmonics which are 'in tune' but not in accordance with equal temperament!
However, that is another story, and suffice it to say that in the keys of C and D major, try to keep the E natural and F sharp respectively, a little flatter.
Continue with these exercises which demand increasingly more difficult steps. Don't go on until the previous exercise is fairly secure.

Now try:

If that was too difficult, then try this way around the problem:

Repeat the above but this time with *diminuendo*:

Finally, do Exercise 1 again, but with changed nuances:

Now go back to the top register exercises bearing these points in mind.

TONE COLOUR

The flute is capable of producing a great variety of sounds, more so than any other orchestral instrument. Musical painting is more interesting when the palette has many colours. These exercises will help you to play in 'technicolor' instead of black and white. Play this first exercise A with a full strong, rich, dark 'purple' tone. Try not to turn the head of the flute inwards to do this. It is better to play this exercise loudly.

Tone Colour—Exercise I

Freely = 60-72 after Reichert

Now play Exercise B with a hollow, 'open', gentle 'yellow' tone, more like the recorder in colour. Play more softly than A.
When changing from A to B try to obtain the greatest *difference* in colour. It is the *difference* in tone which is most important.
The most difficult part is to obtain different colours in the *middle* register. *Be sure that the middle register isn't the same colour for both major and minor sequences, even though the low register is different.*

Play through this sequence of exercises in as many keys as you can, but endeavour eventually to play through all twenty-four keys every day as listed at the end of D. It is better to play the exercise from memory; only write out the remaining keys if you *really* have to – it is better to develop your memory skills at this stage.

Then continue in the following sequence of keys: E flat major; C minor; A flat major; F minor *etc.* through a total of twenty-four keys.

Each key has its own colour and its own problems.

After some weeks – and some success – at Exercise I, practise Exercise II in the same way. The intervals in Exercise II are more widely-spaced which makes it the more difficult.

Remember to make a big difference in tone colour when changing to B.

Then continue in the following sequence of keys: E flat major; C minor; A flat major; F minor *etc.* through a total of twenty-four keys.

Finally, find some books of melodies and practise them using different tone colours. Choose tunes which lend themselves to particular 'colours'. Some examples can be found at the end of this book.

BREATH CONTROL

First consult a good teacher who will put you right about breathing. Otherwise, full explanations with breathing exercises can be found in Practice Book V—BREATHING AND SCALES.

(1) WHISTLE TONES
These are played by blowing the flute in a very *light* and *relaxed* way. They are the notes which sound quietly – and often accidentally – at the end of a diminuendo in the low register. They sound like very quiet squeaks; in fact we often have to practise to avoid them! Try to isolate one of these notes. Finger G natural in the low register to find one of these whistle tones and hold it *for as long as you can* without it 'jumping' or wobbling. Low C natural also produces an easy series of whistle tones. You hardly need any air for these notes. This will help you to control the diaphragm and is equally as good for the lip muscles. A few minutes each day at this exercise will soon show results.

(2) LENGTH
Play middle B natural:

for as long as you can. Check it each day with the second hand of a clock and try to beat your previous day's record. You will soon find ways of exercising economy with the air stream. Within a month you may easily *double* the time for holding this and other notes.

Take care to play the B in tune. It is possible to play a longer note by turning the flute in on the lip and allowing the smaller hole to use less air. Avoid this. It produces a flat, squashed tone and anyway, its cheating!

FLEXIBILITY

To play one note with a good tone is not too difficult and requires the right combination of air speed, air direction, and lip position in relation to the embouchure hole. When moving to another note these ingredients need to change to new values necessary to produce the *second* note with an *equally good tone*. The *changes* and the movements that the lips and air stream have to make from one note to another are what these next exercises are all about. The bigger the interval, the more difficult the changes become. With the right practice you will soon make even large intervals with ease. All the notes should be both beautiful and in tune (*see the exercises on Pitch Control*). Generally the flute sounds louder as it goes up. Do the opposite: practise playing stronger when descending, and softer *but in tune*, when going up. *See preface, note* (*b*)

FLEXIBILITY - I

after Sousseman

roll towards me to make less sharp.

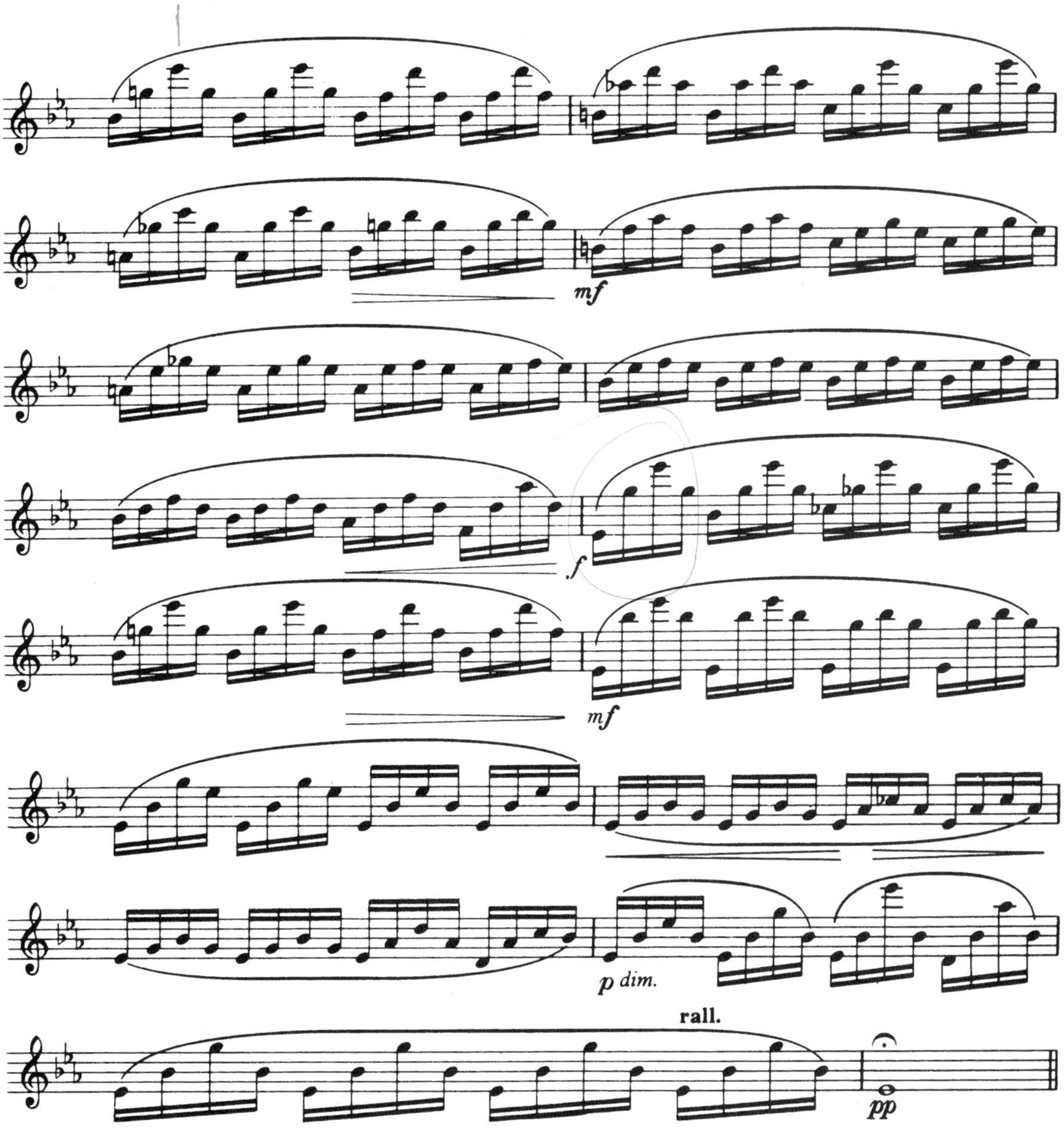

Practise the Flexibility Exercise I firstly like this:

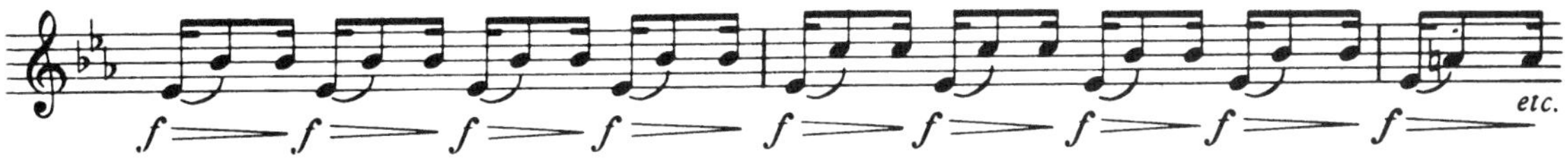

to obtain a good foundation on the low notes, and to check tuning.

Then work up to the G so that it sounds softly, *but not flat*. Try to make the intervals *without strain or undue tension*.

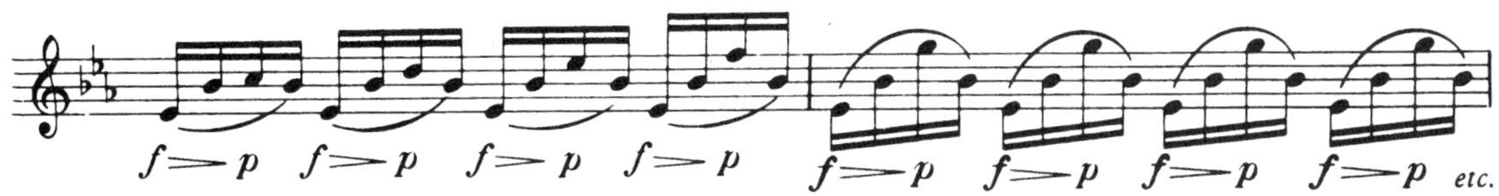

Play the upper notes *softly* and *in tune*.
This may take time.

Then practise the whole exercise in these different ways:

Carefully observe the written nuances. Ask yourself are you playing *really* softly and *really* loudly?

The exercise can be practised in many other ways besides those indicated, including using it as a tone colour exercise.
Tone colour Exercise II can also be used as a *flexibility exercise*.

FLEXIBILITY—II

This is much more difficult and should be attempted only by a more advanced player. The key signature will probably put off less advanced players anyway!

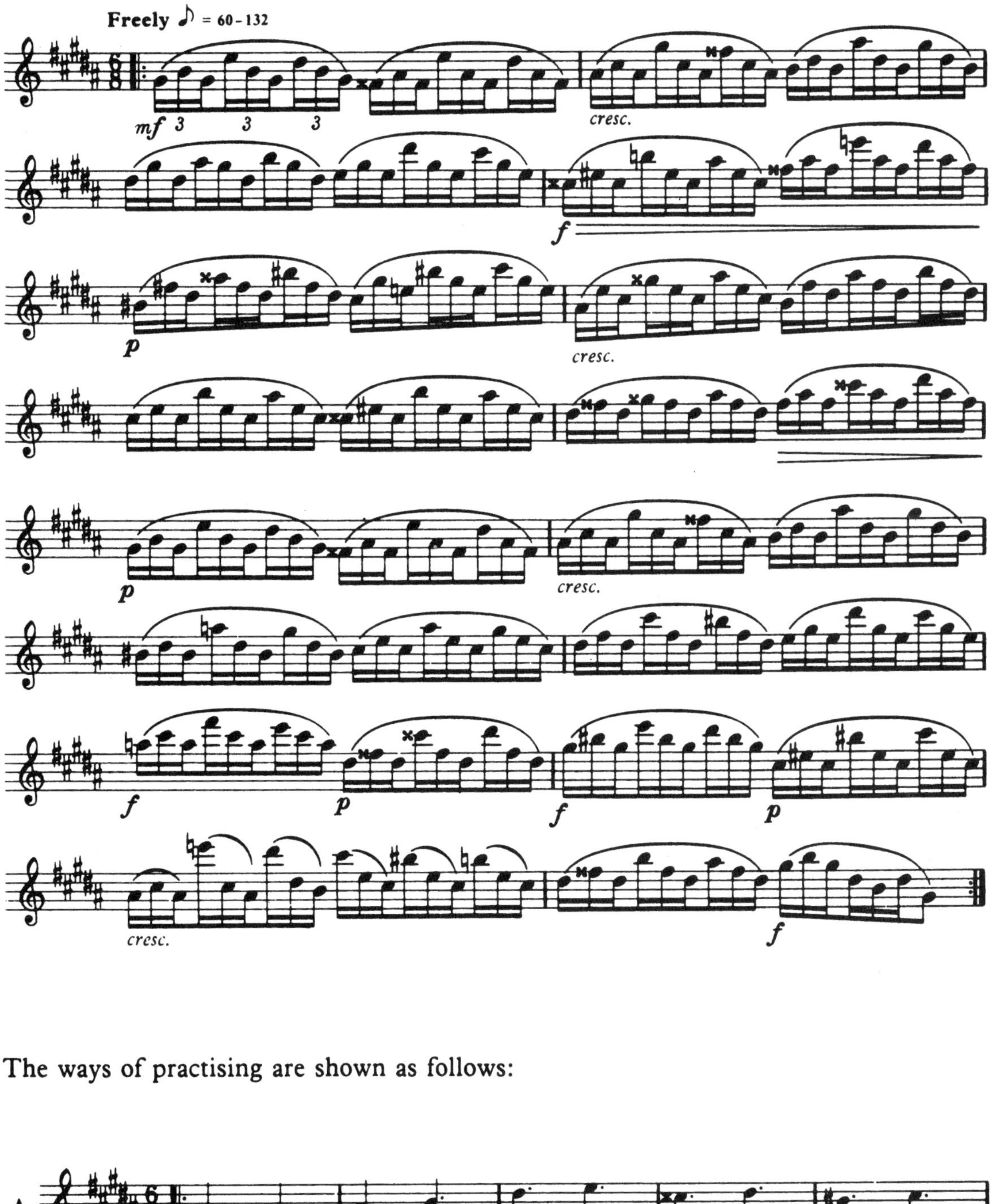
Freely ♪ = 60-132
mf
3 3 3
cresc.
f
p
cresc.
p
cresc.
f
p
f
p
cresc.
f

The ways of practising are shown as follows:

A
mf espressivo
cresc.
f

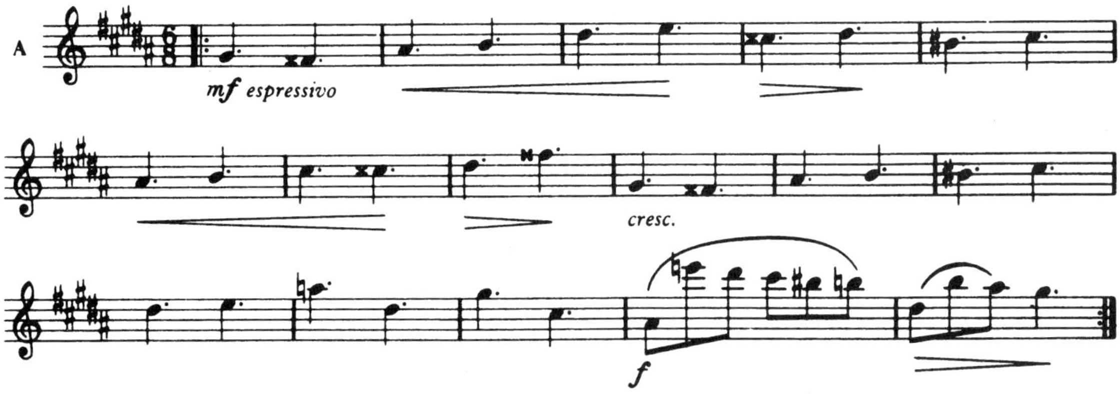

B
mf
cresc.
f
C
mf
3
D
mf
3
E
mf
3
F
mf
3

Most studies and pieces can be subjected to this kind of practice which is most valuable and beneficial. And interesting!

Some examples from the flute repertoire illustrating flexibility difficulties can be found at the end of the book.

PROBLEMS BOX

1) The exercises are tiring? They certainly are! Be sure to warm up your lips and muscles before practising these exercises. Remember the athlete spends hours warming up before the race or before the practice.
2) Difficulties with intonation? See the *Pitch Control* section.
3) Don't worry about making a lot of movement with jaw/lips initially. Produce a good result *by whatever means* and then reduce the movements without losing what you have gained.

PITCH CONTROL – I

MOBILITY

Playing in tune is inseparable from a beautiful musical performance. This section on pitch control covers the problems of playing loudly and softly, of diminuendos and crescendos without becoming flatter or sharper.

1) Play the C natural fortissimo and at the same time make a diminuendo *without making any corrective movements* with the lips, jaw or head.
The note will go flat.

2) Now play the same C natural, but this time try to *bend* the note both up and down by moving your lips and jaw forward and, if the note won't move enough, also raise your head. *Do not* move your hands, arms or flute to do this.

Before practising loud and soft playing, and diminuendos and crescendos, you will need to obtain enough mobility to enable you to alter the pitch easily and at will. Next, then, practise this jazzy exercise. Do not finger the third note of each bar; make the semitones by bending the pitch downwards.

PITCH CONTROL—II

NOTE ENDINGS AND NUANCES

It becomes obvious that, as the air speed is reduced (diminuendo) the blow-hole of the flute needs to be correspondingly uncovered in order to remain at the same pitch. These movements of the blowing, together with the lips, jaw and head need to be practised together carefully so as to make perfect diminuendos and crescendos. *Do* count, carefully.

Now try Exercise 2. When you reach the note D *, the pitch is more difficult to 'bend'. Right-hand notes are more difficult to 'bend' than left-hand notes because the tube is longer. The open C sharp is the most moveable note, as we all know, and the most difficult to stabilize.

After several days, or longer, on the first two exercises, go on to Exercise 3, 4, 5 and 6 but don't do the next until the previous exercise is faultless. The reason is plainly clear. The process of co-ordinating both the release of the breath and the lips/jaw/head movement is speeded up until, at Excercise 6 – a 'short ending' – the movement is very quick indeed. This movement should eventually become automatic.

It will be clearly seen that:

(a) there is much to be gained by practising the first three exercises *reversing the nuances;*
(b) it is the method by which the pitch in loud and soft playing, as in 'phrasing' is controlled;
(c) that even loud sustained notes should have a 'short ending' on the end of them.
(d) as you become more proficient, the movement, particularly of the head, will become less.

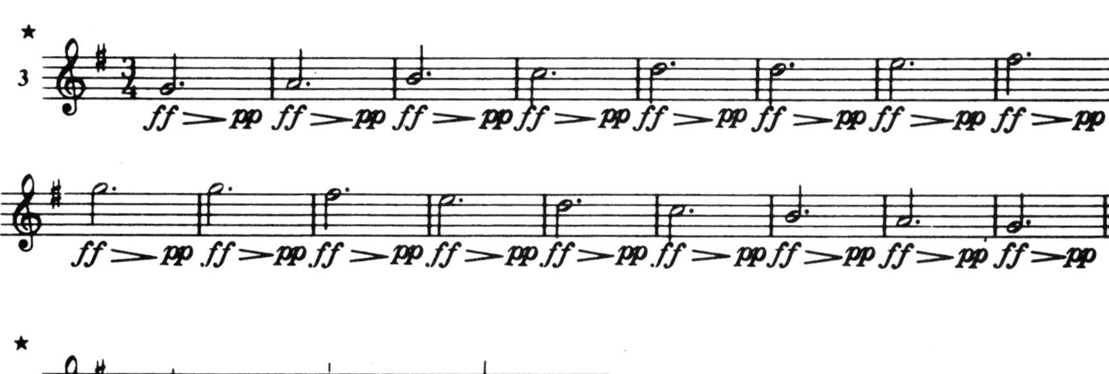

'SHORT ENDINGS'

Use your new-found technique in Exercises 7 and 8 but be sure to play *really* softly and *really* loudly maintaining the same pitch.

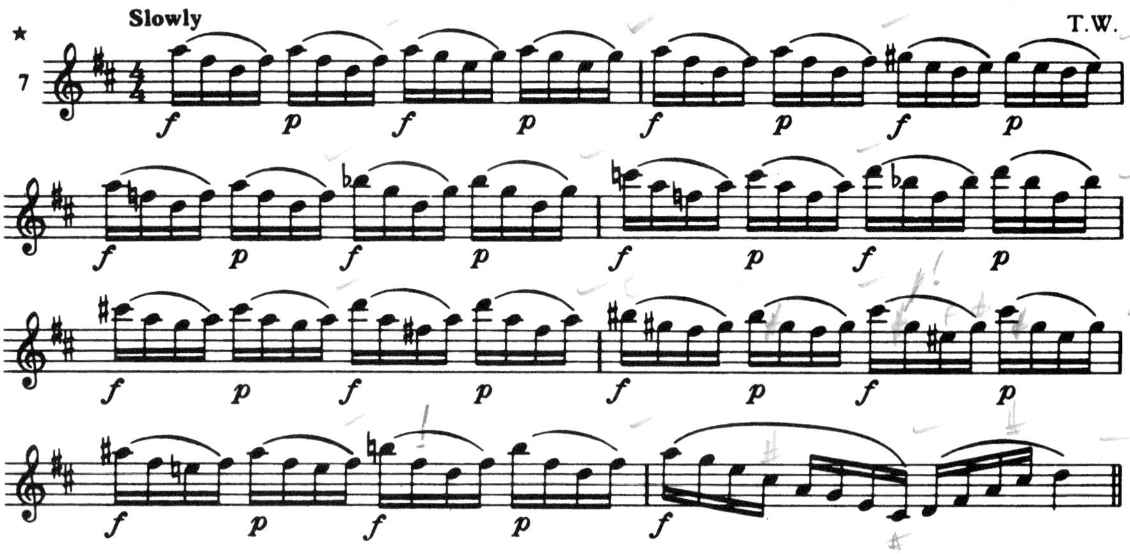

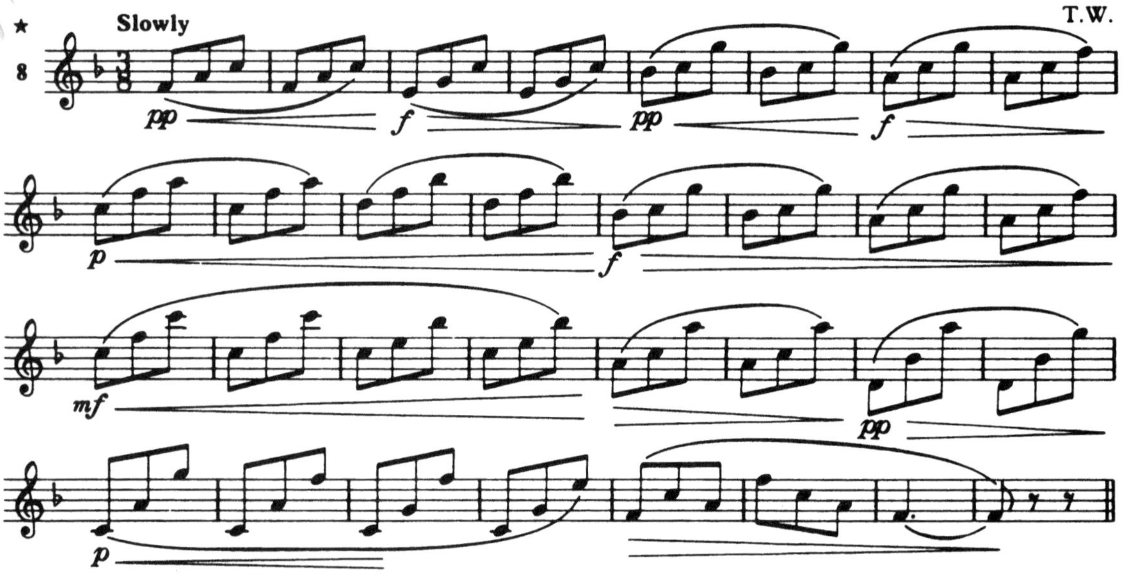

* 7 **Slowly** T.W.

f *p* *f* *p* *f* *p* *f* *p*

* 8 **Slowly** T.W.

pp *f* *pp* *f*

p *f*

mf *pp*

p

PROBLEMS BOX

1 Never, at this stage, end the notes with your tongue or by shutting your lips together. Use 'endings' to end notes.
2 Don't move the flute inwards or outwards with the hands; use only lips, jaw or head to change the pitch.
3 The end of the note is flat? Move lips, jaw or head more!
4 When the notes get wispy (see Breath Control (I) Whistle tones) push the lips forward more to *stop* them sounding.
5 Check your tuning both before and during practice with a *reliable* piano, tuning fork or tuning meter.

INTONATION*

These exercises will help you control the pitch and tone of both C natural and C sharp and the trill key notes.
First check the pitch of C sharp against the second harmonic, or overtone, of low C sharp. Do the same for C natural.
Then compare the pitch of the upper C sharp with the third harmonic, or overtone, of low F sharp and the fourth harmonic of low C sharp.
Do the same with C natural and F natural.

In Exercises 1 and 1a be sure that the two Cs in the second bar—one harmonic and one natural—are at the same pitch.

Do the same with Exercises 2 and 2a.
Practise *both* these exercises every day before attempting Exercise 3.

Exercise 3 Here you will make a much quicker comparison between the overtone and the natural note. They must both sound at the *same* pitch.

* A fuller and more detailed study is to be found in Practice Book IV – INTONATION AND VIBRATO.

Exercises 4 and 5 Endeavour to make these rather spineless trill key notes as beefy as the natural notes. It will take a lot of practice but well worth it. Note the fingering:

1 – finger C plus first trill key = D natural
2 – finger C plus second trill key = E flat

Exercises 6 and 7 Play these as though you are using *normal* fingering. Try to be convincing. Note the fingering:

1 – finger C sharp plus 1st trill key = D
2 – finger C sharp plus 2nd trill key = D sharp

Repeat using trill fingerings and normal fingerings alternately.

Exercise 8 Normal fingering is used in this exercise, the point of which is to ensure that C natural and D flat are properly in tune and with a good tone.

Exercise 9 As in the previous exercise. You may find that a flatter C sharp* than in Exercise 8 sounds better in this key, but ensure that E natural is not flattened as well!

If you need more exercises, practise Flexibility I and II.

Some examples from the solo repertoire will be found on page 42. See also Practice Book IV—INTONATION and VIBRATO; the twenty-four studies in that book – one in every key – are invaluable for intonation and phrasing practice.

Finally, remember that the exercises in this book on tone, pitch control and flexibility are all interlinked and dependent on each other. Each must be considered with reference to the others when practising.

**The finer points of playing correctly both at equal temperament and to mean-tone tuning will be discussed in* Vol. IV—INTONATION and VIBRATO.

EXAMPLES

Here are some extracts from the flute repertoire which illustrate the various points raised in this book.

TONE COLOUR

These are examples where the imaginative flautist will endeavour to capture the intentions of the composer through use of tone colour.

SICILIENNE — FAURE

★

MADRIGAL — P. GAUBERT[1]

Here, the colours can be changed to suit the keys through which the melody passes.

PAVANE — FAURE

★

[1]Reproduced by permission of Enoch et Cie—Paris, UK and Commonwealth agents Edwin Ashdown Ltd.

L'Après-midi is also a good test of breath control. At the very first performance, three flautists were engaged to play the solo in unison because of the breathing problem. Today, it is usual to play it in one breath.

PRÉLUDE À L'APRÈS-MIDI D'UN FAUNE — DEBUSSY

DANSE MACABRE — SAINT-SAENS

SINFONIA FROM CANTATA 156 — J. S. BACH

Show the keys by the colour of your tone.

FLEXIBILITY

These extracts show that the wide intervals should be made easily: practice, without undue tension, will give that ease.

SONATE EN CONCERT J-M. DAMASE[1]

SICILIENNE

PITCH CONTROL

Note Endings The flute repertoire, both solo and orchestral, abounds with examples of difficult diminuendos whilst striving to stay in tune. Although these pieces are without accompaniment, nevertheless, good intonation is essential. To go flat at the end of any of these works will cause the music to go sour. Check the last few notes with a *reliable* piano.

SYRINX DEBUSSY

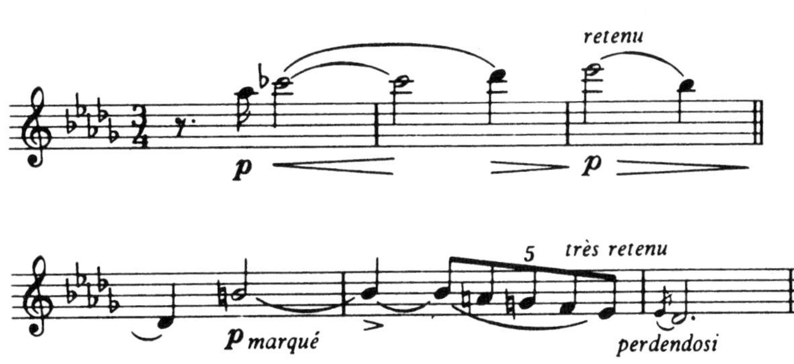

PIÈCE IBERT[2]

DANSE DE LA CHÈVRE: HONEGGER[3]

[1]Editions Lemoine, Paris/United Music Publishers Ltd. By permission.
[2]Extract from J. Ibert's *Piece for Flute*. Copyright by Alphonse Leduc & Cie Paris. Owners and publishers for all countries.
[3]Copyright Editions Salabert. Used by permission.

TREVOR WYE

OMNIBUS
EDITION
BOOKS 1-5

PRACTICE BOOKS for the *flute*

VOLUME 2
Technique

CONTENTS

TECHNIQUE—GENERAL

Regular practice is most important to progress in technique. Time lost cannot be made up the next day. If an athlete misses two days of training, he doesn't try, in one day, to make up for all the time he has lost. He would soon pull a muscle.
Work *regularly* at technique.
Work for longer at the keys you find most difficult.
Whatever time is available to you for practice, about one third should be spent on these exercises.
Work hardest at the weakest fingers.
When a difficulty arises, repeat the difficult bar *four more times.*
In all the exercises:—
(a) maintain a good posture. Never sit down.
(b) use a good tone.
(c) play with clockwork precision.
(d) try to keep your fingers close to the keys.
It cannot be too strongly emphasised that technical progress is a question of *time, patience* and *intelligent work.*

TECHNIQUE

The finger muscles need constant practice to achieve (a) independence from each other and (b) speed. Scales are essential to this aim, but *only* when played from the tonic or keynote to the top of the compass, then down to the lowest note on the flute and back again to the keynote:

One-octave scales, or scales over a twelfth, are not much good; your time would more profitably be spent elsewhere. Scales over the whole compass, *played slowly,* are within the reach of most young players. True, most local examinations require scales over one octave or a twelfth. This is to keep in line with all the other instruments. The flute fingering is easier than the clarinet, oboe and bassoon and it is easier to play fast in all keys on the flute. Therefore you should aim at the ideal of exercising your fingers and brain over the whole range of the flute from low C to high B *in all keys.* In preparation for these scales, therefore, the following exercises are important. Before starting, it would be a good plan to exercise the weakest fingers—the right hand third finger and little finger—and to stretch the little finger so that low C sharp and C natural can be played without it straightening. *Always bend the little finger.* If necessary, use it on its *right* side. Play this exercise using the little finger on the C sharp *key* —the one with the pad in—to play C sharp! *Try not to move your hand.*

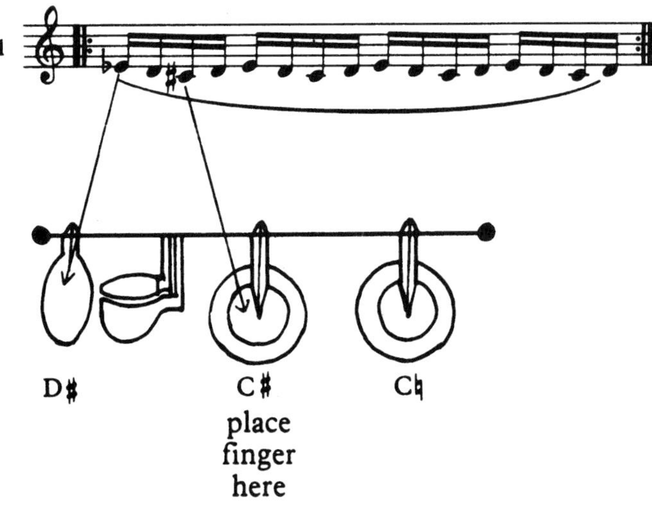

Repeat this exercise many times during your practice. Then change the E flat to an E natural but *make sure you use your D sharp key for E natural!*
Remember, too, to slide your little finger when required. Rub the tip of your little finger along the side of your nose; it will gather skin oil and will slide on the keys more easily.

Here are some more:

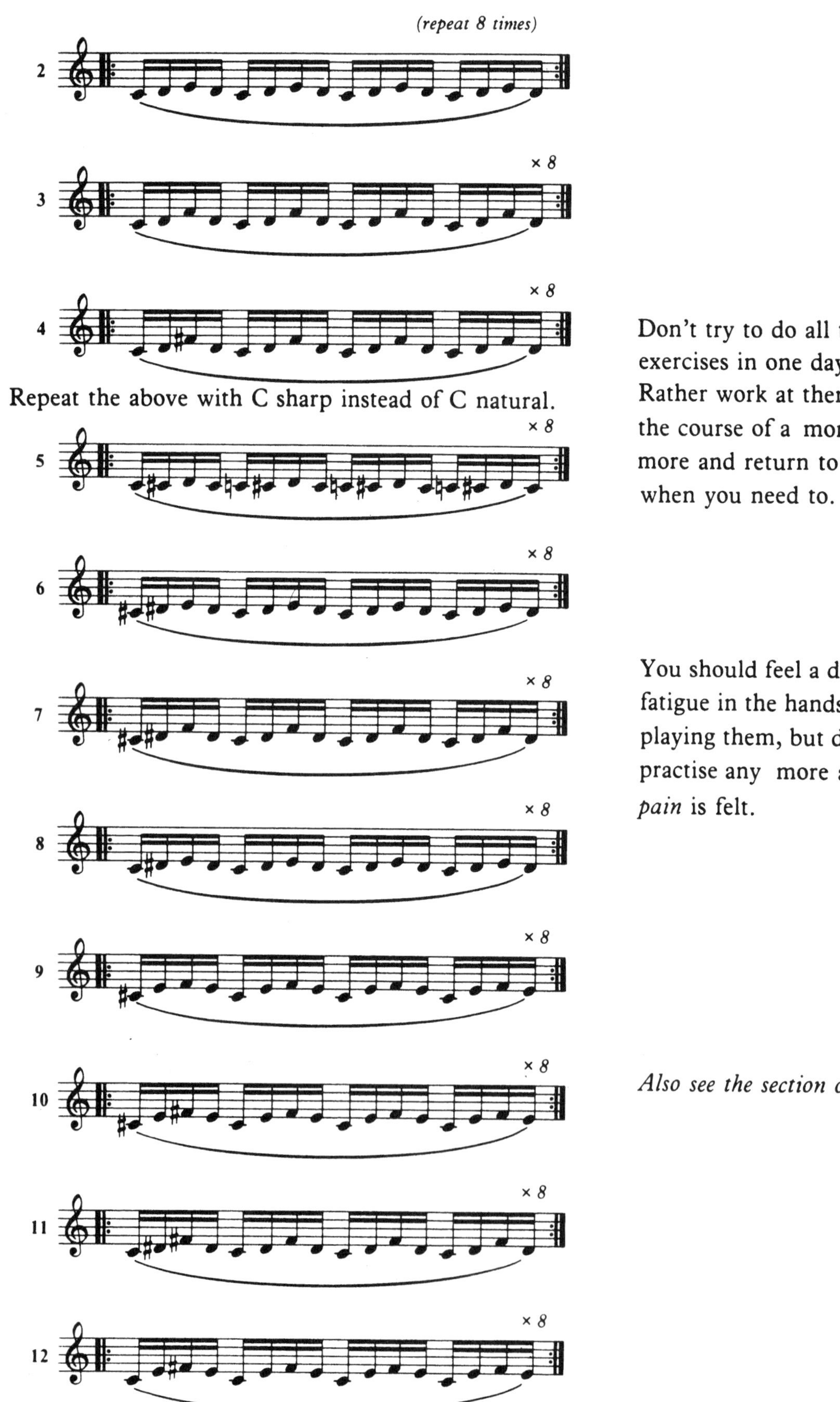

Repeat the above with C sharp instead of C natural.

Don't try to do all these exercises in one day. Rather work at them over the course of a month or more and return to them when you need to.

You should feel a distinct fatigue in the hands after playing them, but don't practise any more after *pain* is felt.

Also see the section on relaxing.

Now commence the Daily Exercises I remembering the following points:

(a) strive for evenness; play like clockwork.
(b) always use the 'correct' fingering, i.e. (1) middle E flat with first finger off; (2) F sharp always with third finger right hand; (3) use D sharp key for every note except low and middle D natural (and low C natural and C sharp) and the very top B natural and C.
(c) always use the most difficult fingering, i.e. B flat with the first finger of the right hand. *See preface, note (b)*
(d) play the exercises with a *good tone.*
(e) practise them every day.

> **PROBLEMS BOX**
>
> When you have difficulty playing—with the correct fingering!—two or three notes together, then the numbers at the end of each line refer to the Scale Exercises which follow; these will help you overcome your particular problem. After a time, it will no longer be necessary to refer to these exercises as they are quite self-explanatory. They back up points (b) and (c) in the preface.

DAILY EXERCISES—I

MAJOR

A1: B1: C1: B21:
B24: C20: C24.

A2: B2: C2:
A12: B3: C3.

A3: B3: C3:
A13: B12: C8.

A4: B4: C4:
A5: B5: C5.

A5: B5: C5:
C24: D5: E4.

A16: B6: C6.

A7: B7: C7:
D16: E11: F10.

A8: B8: C8. etc.

By referring to the Scale Exercises, it will be clear how to work at the remainder of the Daily Exercises and will help you to invent new ways of overcoming your technical problems. Write in the scale exercise numbers yourself in the right-hand column if you wish.

Be sure to finger E flat with the first finger off, and use the D sharp key for E natural. In case of difficulty, some E flat exercises can be found in VOL. III—ARTICULATION.

Now go back to the sign * and continue one octave higher as far as you can. If your familiarity with the upper register is limited, try to include one *new* line each week. You will soon reach all the upper notes.

DAILY EXERCISES—II

MINOR

*

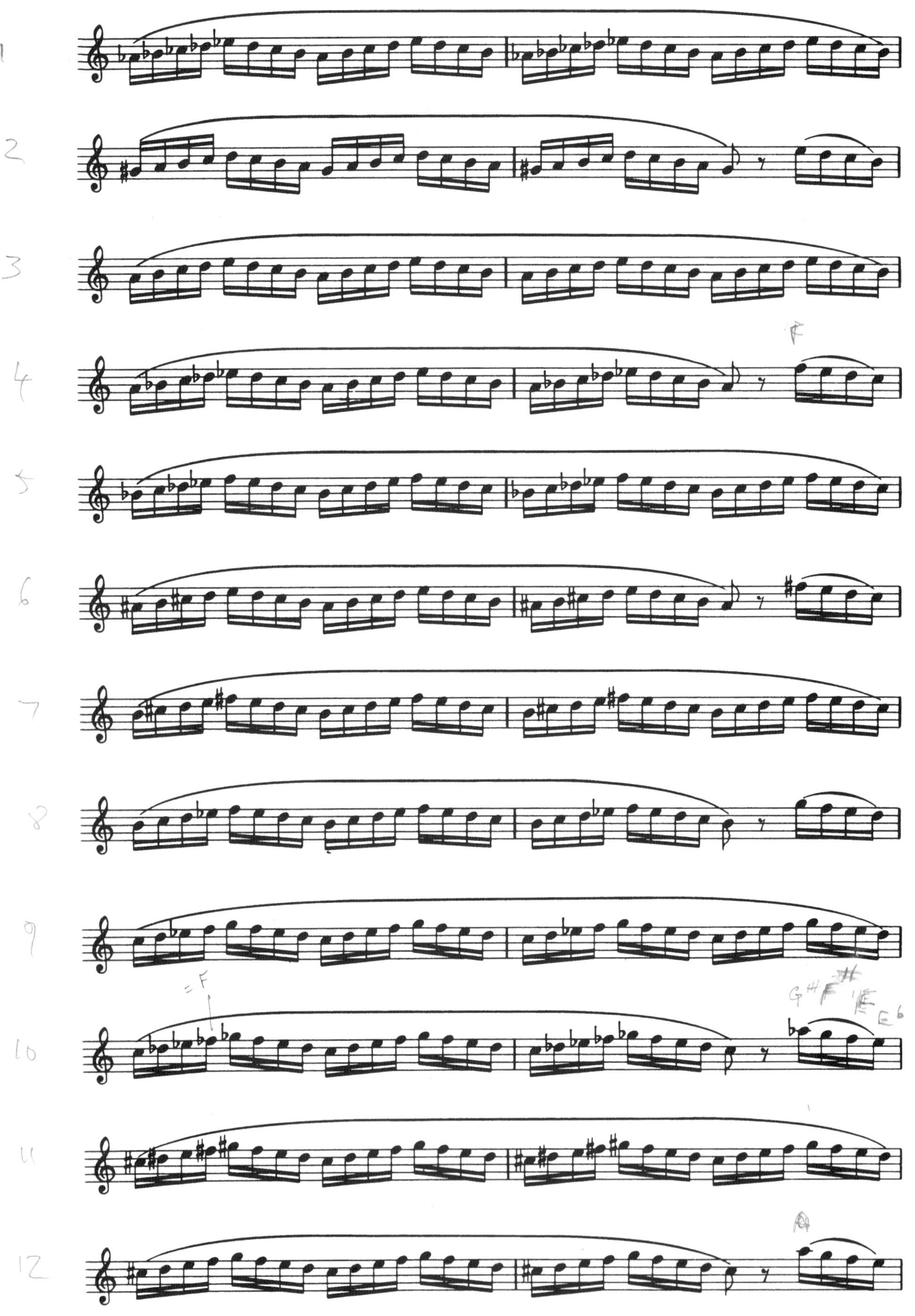

Be sure to finger E flat with the first finger off, and use the D sharp key for E natural. In case of difficulty, some E flat exercises can be found in VOL. III—ARTICULATION.

Now go back to the sign * and continue one octave higher as far as you can. If your familiarity with the upper register is limited, try to include one *new* line each week. You will soon reach all the upper notes.

> **PROBLEM BOX**
>
> Where any uneveness or difficulty occurs, remember to use the appropriate Scale Exercises to help isolate and overcome the problem. See preface note (c).

SCALE EXERCISES

Perhaps, so far, you have used these scale exercises only as a remedy for technical difficulties in the Daily Exercises. If so, now practise them as exercises in their own right. They are most valuable. DON'T GET DISHEARTENED. Remember that these are CONCENTRATED exercises. You will achieve much quicker technical results with these studies than in books full of pretty Victorian studies.
Keep at them!

SCALE EXERCISES

SERIES A: MAJOR

Repeat the whole one octave higher and then two octaves higher as far as No. 7. Be sure to finger E flat with the first finger off, and use the D sharp key for E natural. In case of difficulty, some E flat exercises can be found in VOL. III—ARTICULATION.

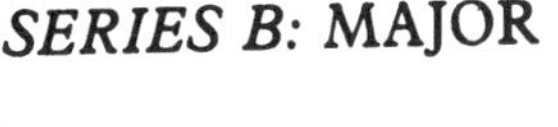

SERIES B: MAJOR

1 2

3 4

5 6

7 8

9 10

11 12

13 14

15 16

17 18

19
20
21
22
23
24

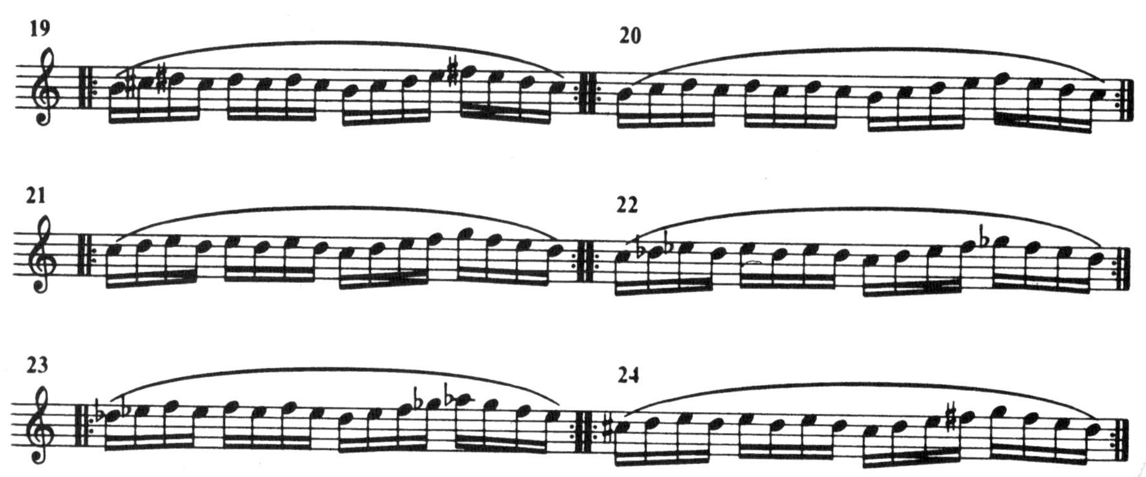

Repeat the whole one octave higher and then two octaves higher as far as No. 7. Be sure to finger E flat with the first finger off, and use the D sharp key for E natural. In case of difficulty, some E flat exercises can be found in VOL. III—ARTICULATION.

SERIES C: MAJOR

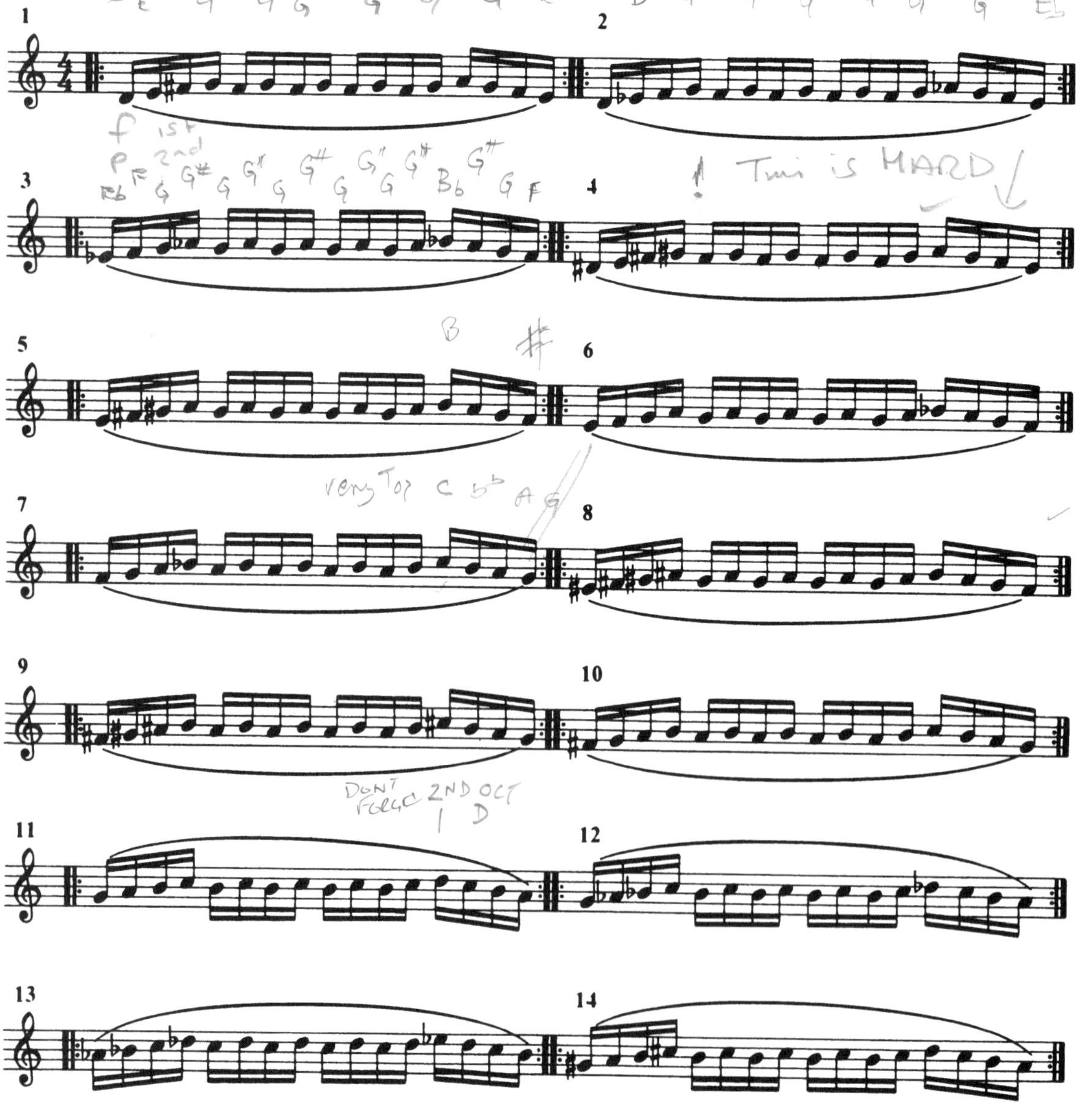

1
2
3
4
5
6
7
8
9
10
11
12
13
14

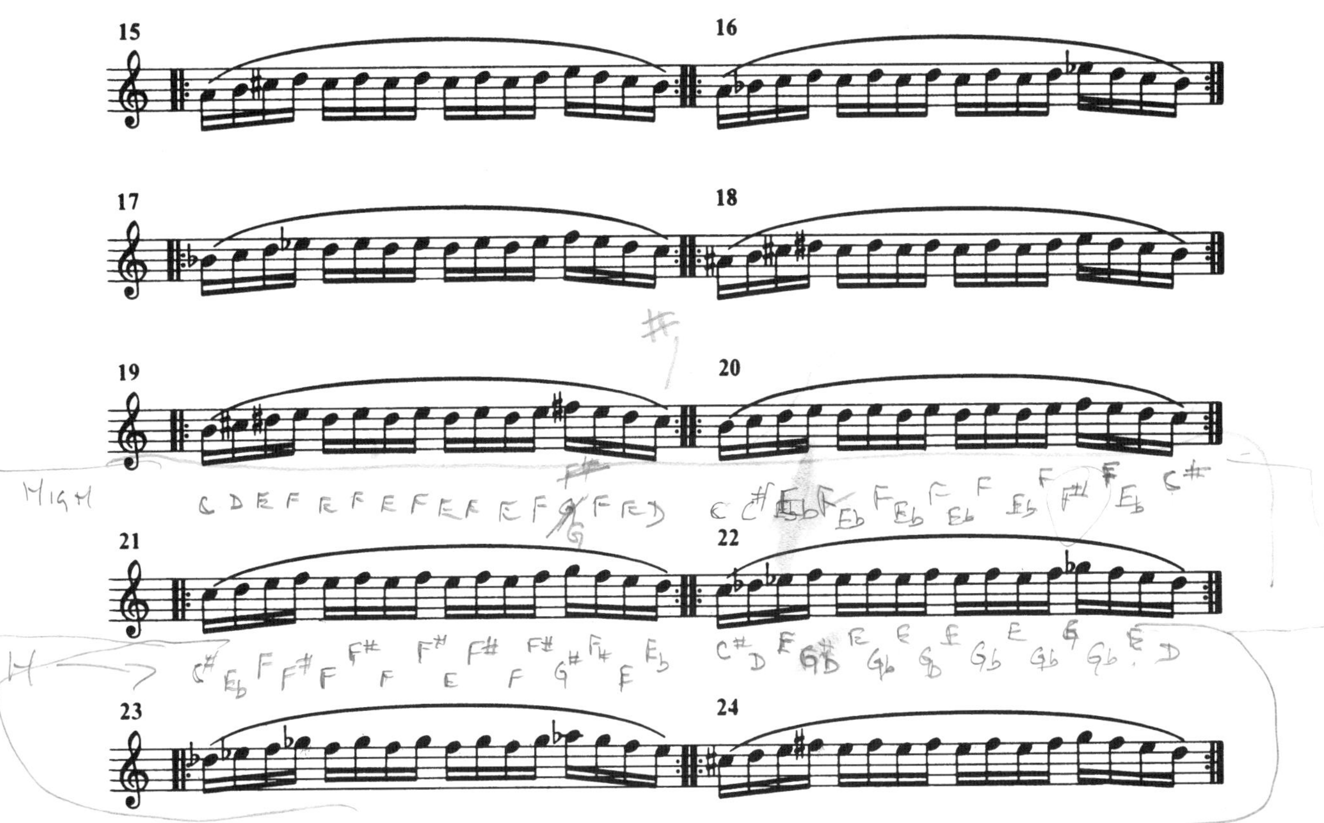

Repeat the whole one octave higher and then two octaves higher as far as No. 7.

SERIES D: MINOR

Repeat the whole one octave higher and then two octaves higher as far as No. 7. Be sure to finger E flat with the first finger off, and use the D sharp key for E natural. In case of difficulty, some E flat exercises can be found in VOL. III—ARTICULATION.

SERIES E: MINOR

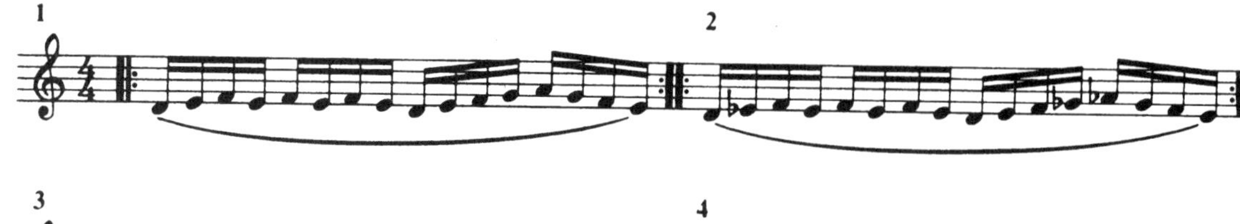

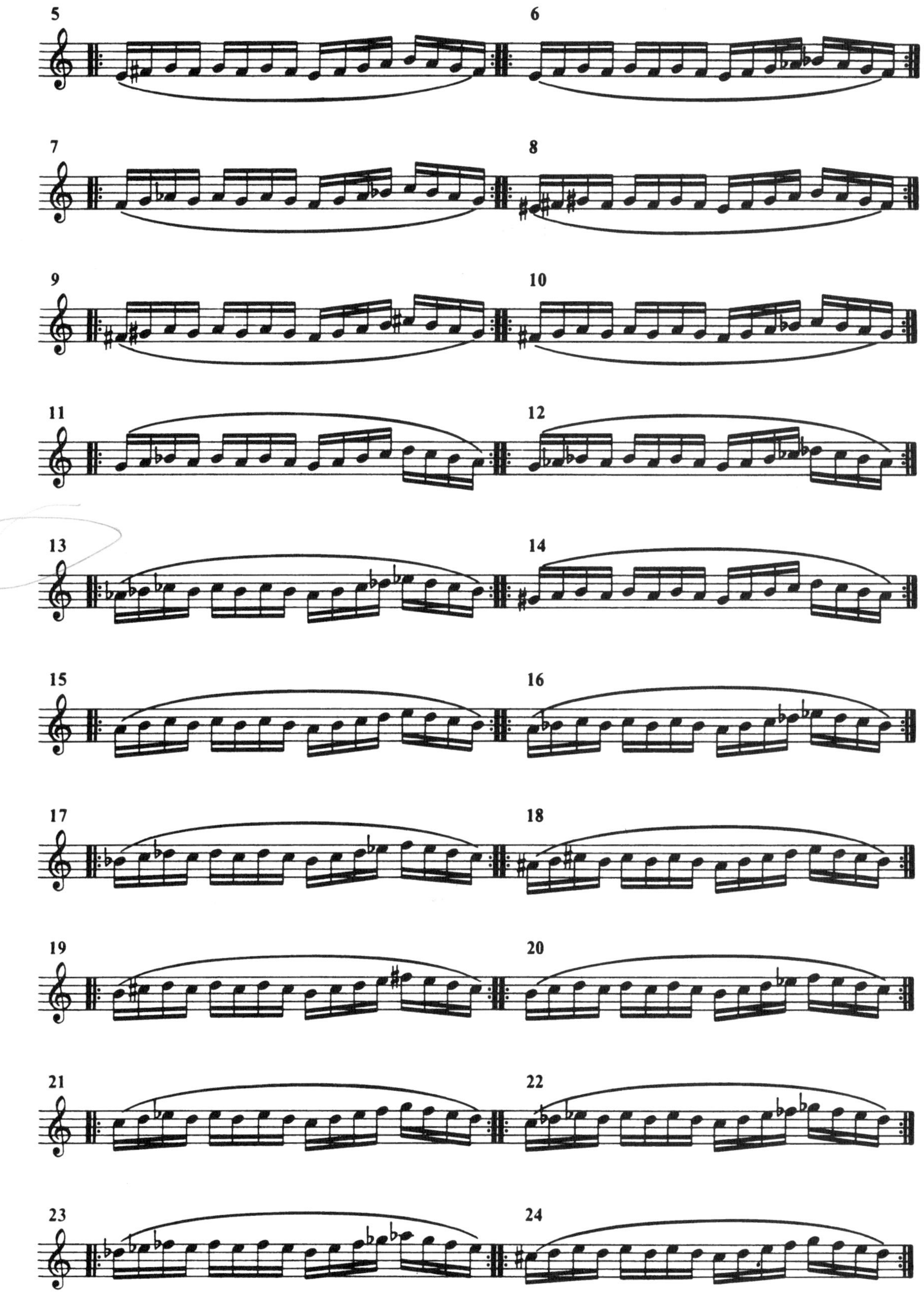

Repeat the whole one octave higher and then two octaves higher as far as No. 7.

SERIES F: MINOR

Repeat the whole exercise one octave higher and then two octaves higher as far as No. 7.

DAILY EXERCISES—II

Practise these exercises *every day*. A short period every day *will* achieve results. Once a week at them will not. Unless you intend to live as long as Methuselah: he lived 969 years.

MAJOR

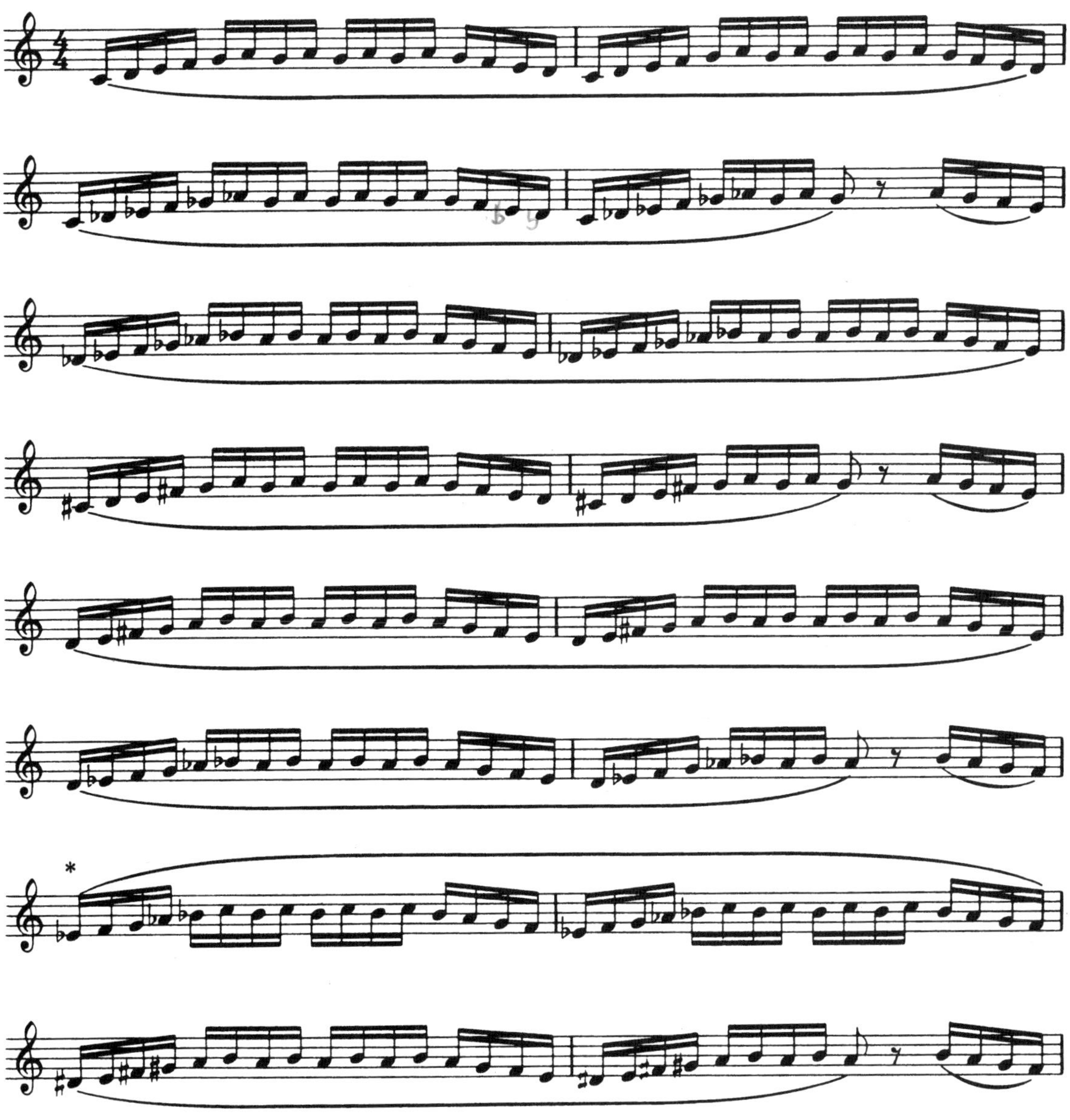

*

Go back to the sign * and repeat one octave higher to the end.

MINOR

Go back to the sign * and repeat one octave higher to the end.

MACHIAVELLIAN EXERCISES*

These two exercises are difficult. However, following your acceptance of the preface—(b) and (c)—take pleasure in the difficulties encountered.

The Machiavellian exercises are hard, but do remember that it is really concentrated stuff. You will find just *one* of these bars wrapped up in many a pretty nineteenth-century study. But the practice—and the mastery—of that one bar was really the point of the whole study!

MACHIAVELLIAN EXERCISES—I

*Machiavelli (1469-1527): A Florentine statesman who had a reputation for craftiness and guile.

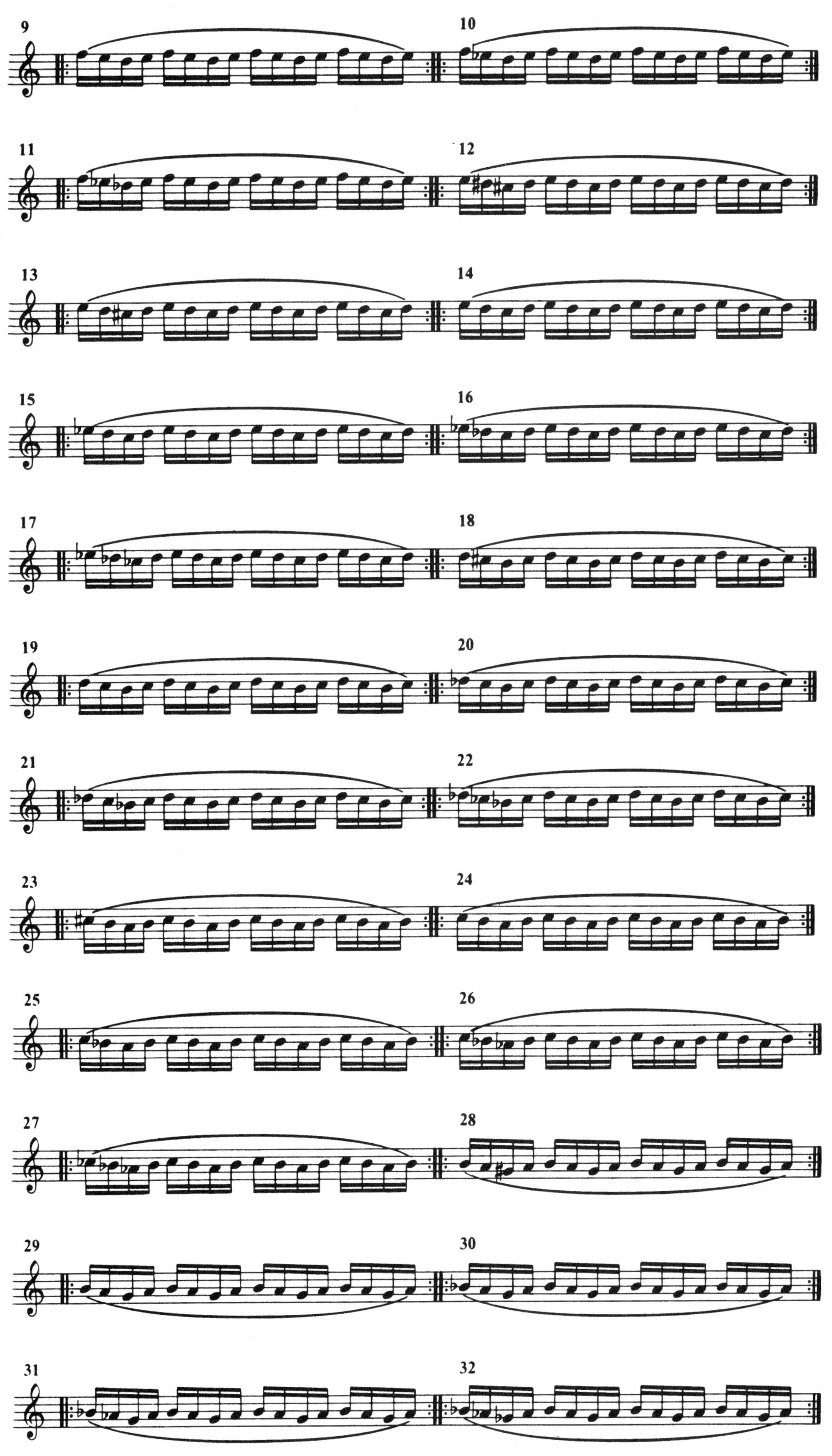
9
10
11
12
13
14
15
16
17
18
19
20
21
22
23
24
25
26
27
28
29
30
31
32

Repeat Nos. 1-20 one octave higher. Be sure to finger E flat with the first finger off, and use the D sharp key for E natural. In case of difficulty, some E flat exercises can be found in VOL. III—ARTICULATION.

Now repeat the exercise as a *continuous* study; i.e. without repeating each bar.

MACHIAVELLIAN EXERCISES—II

MACHIAVELLIAN EXERCISES—II is more difficult, but it *can* be fun. Roll your sleeves up and go to it, but always remember to practise it with:—
(a) clockwork evenness
(b) correct fingering
(c) good tone.

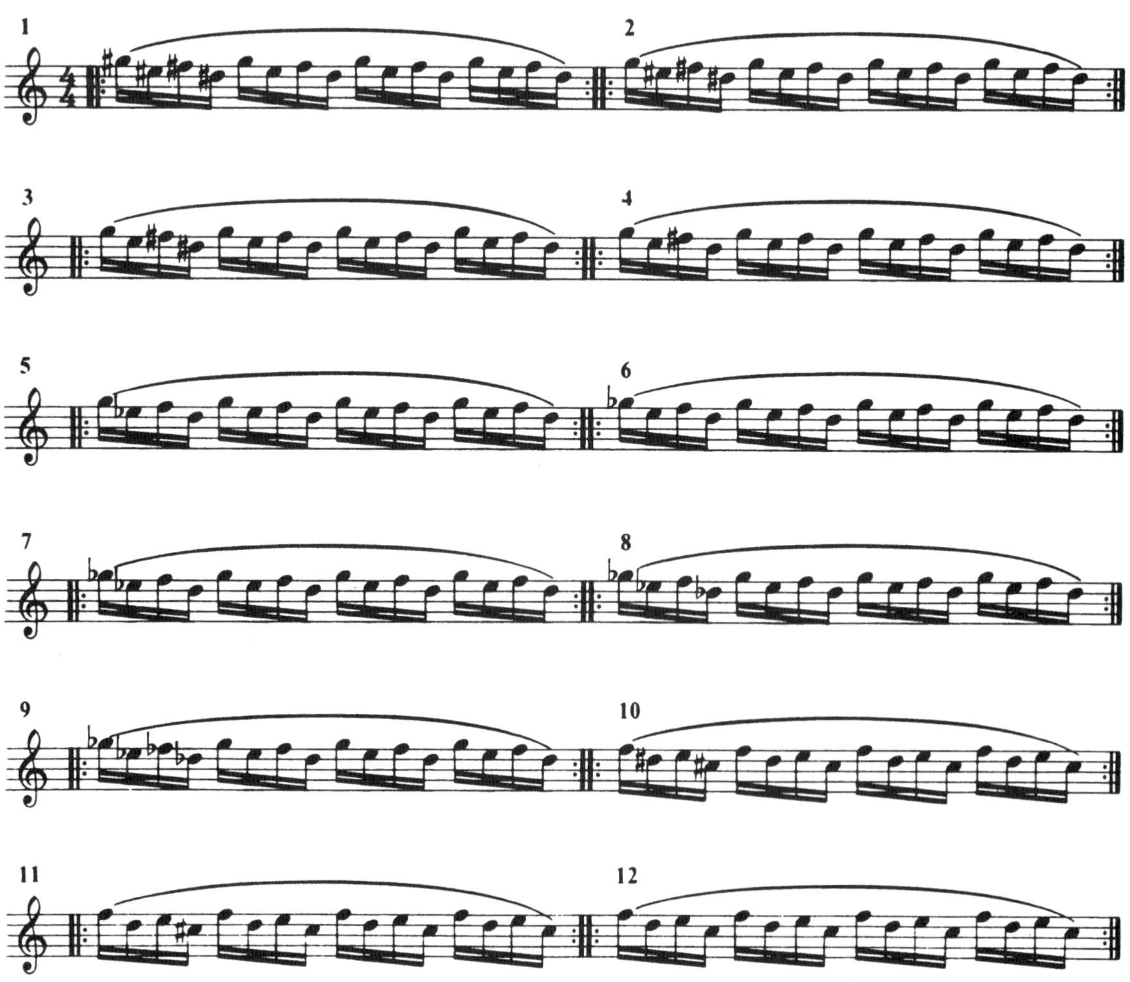

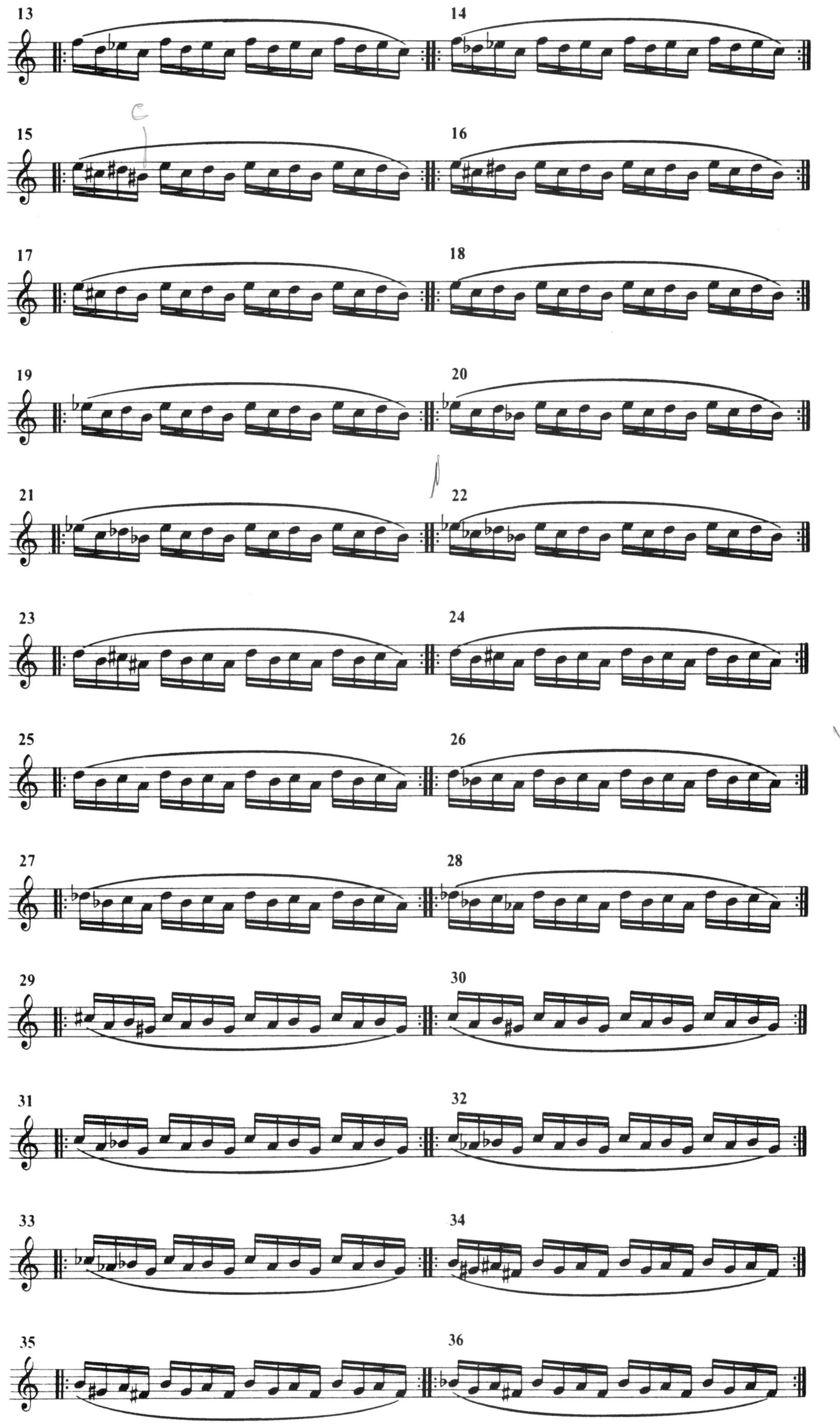
13
14
15
16
17
18
19
20
21
22
23
24
25
26
27
28
29
30
31
32
33
34
35
36

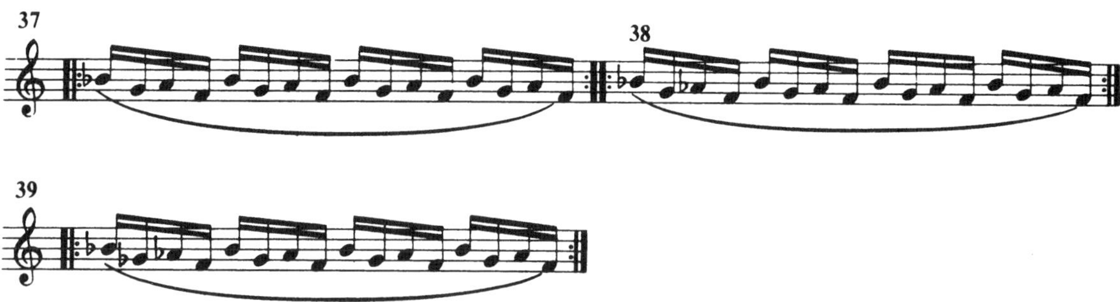

Repeat Nos. 1-26 one octave higher.

Technique: examples of difficult passages abound; you will find three examples at the end of the book.

Now repeat the exercise as a *continuous* study; i.e. without repeating each bar.

RELAXING

Choose some paperback books of the same thickness as the width of your hand. Lie down on the floor with knees raised and slightly apart. Place the books under your head with hands and arms to the side. You will notice an arch in the small of the back; this will gradually disappear. It usually takes about five minutes to assume contact with the floor. As it does you will feel your spine becoming a little longer and will probably want to move your hips down a little. Remain like this for at least ten minutes.

This relaxing position is used by many artists, both actors and musicians to loosen up and relax before going on stage.

When undergoing long tiring hours of instrumental practice, you will find it helpful to relax both during and after these sessions. It is particularly useful to counteract the tensions which can result when practising technically difficult studies such as the exercises for low C sharp and the little finger of the right hand, and the Machiavellian Exercises.

TRILLS

Most players avoid trill studies. They are difficult but *most important* for the development of a fine technique.

Before commencing, note carefully the following points:

(a) even when playing slowly, move the finger *quickly* up and down. Pat the keys going down and pat the air coming up!

(b) be *really* rhythmic in this exercise. Play exactly the right number of notes in the right time.

(c) always make a good tone on *both* notes when trilling, especially when using the trill keys or other 'weak' notes. See also VOL. I—TONE.

(d) don't move the *hand* whilst trilling. *See preface, note (d)*

EXAMPLE

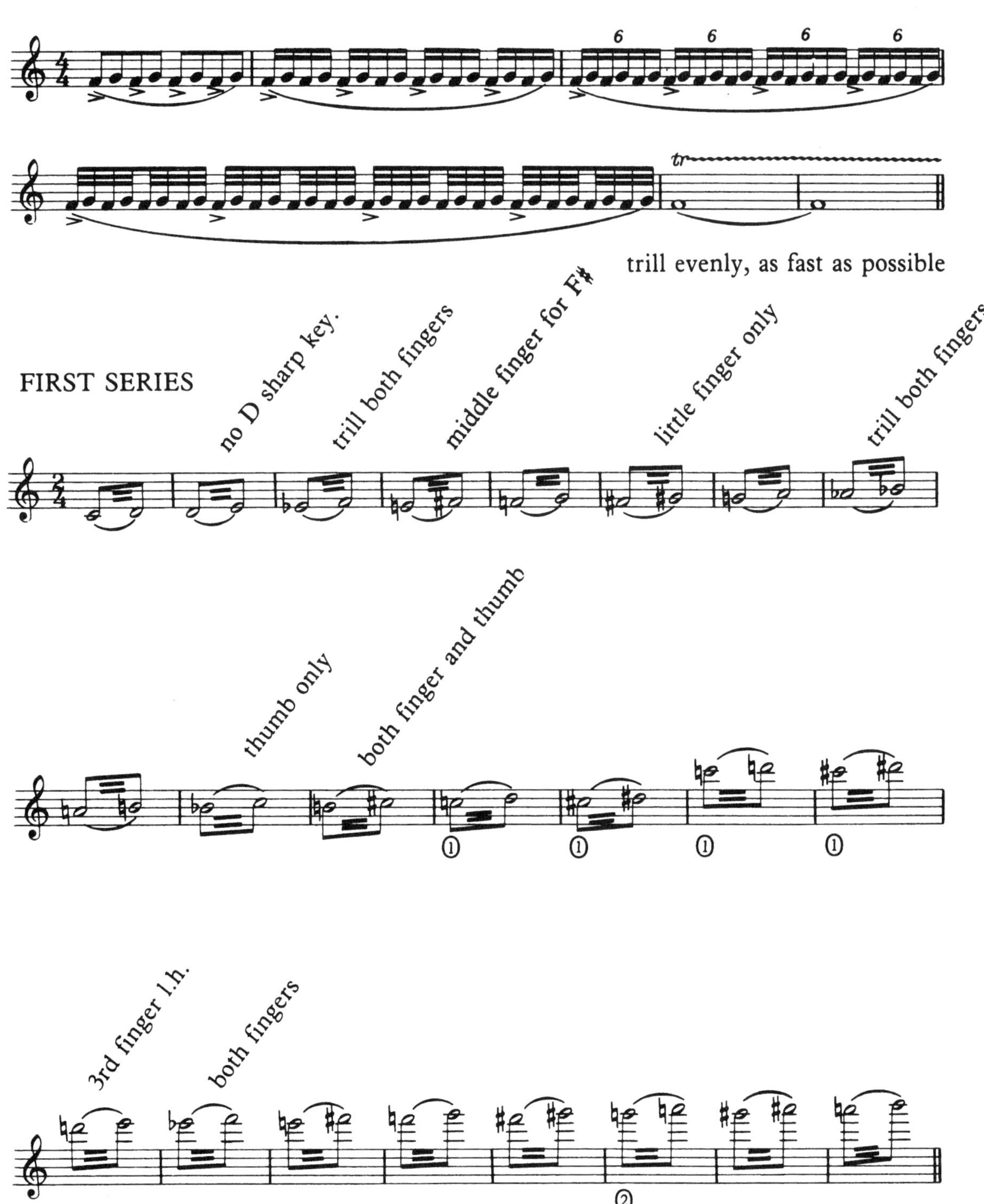

①Check these trills in the trill exercises found in VOL. 1—TONE.

②If you can't find a satisfactory trill for this note, finger top G natural and trill the first finger of the left hand and the first trill key *alternately*.
Practise it; it really works!

PROBLEM BOX

If any discomfort is felt in wrist, arm, shoulder or neck whilst practising trill exercises, consult your teacher regarding posture. Also try the relaxing exercise.

★Exercises for the *tone* of trills and for C sharp can be found in VOL. I – TONE, on p.37.

SEQUENCES

These exercises help sight-reading, improvisation, the reflexes and your memory. The problem we all find with sight-reading is not so much not being able to play the notes, but responding *quickly* enough to the written notes, especially if there are some difficult accidentals!
These sequences will also enable those who are keen on baroque music or jazz to get to know the flute well enough to be able to improvise – a most useful accomplishment and one to which many an orchestral player has had to resort when he has lost his place!
Play through this first exercise. Later, try not to read the notes; play from memory if you can. If you aren't very familiar with the extreme top of the compass, find the way to come down with elegance. Like a mountain, go up only as far as you can!
More exercises for improvisation can be found in VOL. 5 – BREATHING AND SCALES.

MAJOR

Now practise the same exercise again with these different rhythms:

The minor form is not so easy and may take a little longer to master:

MINOR

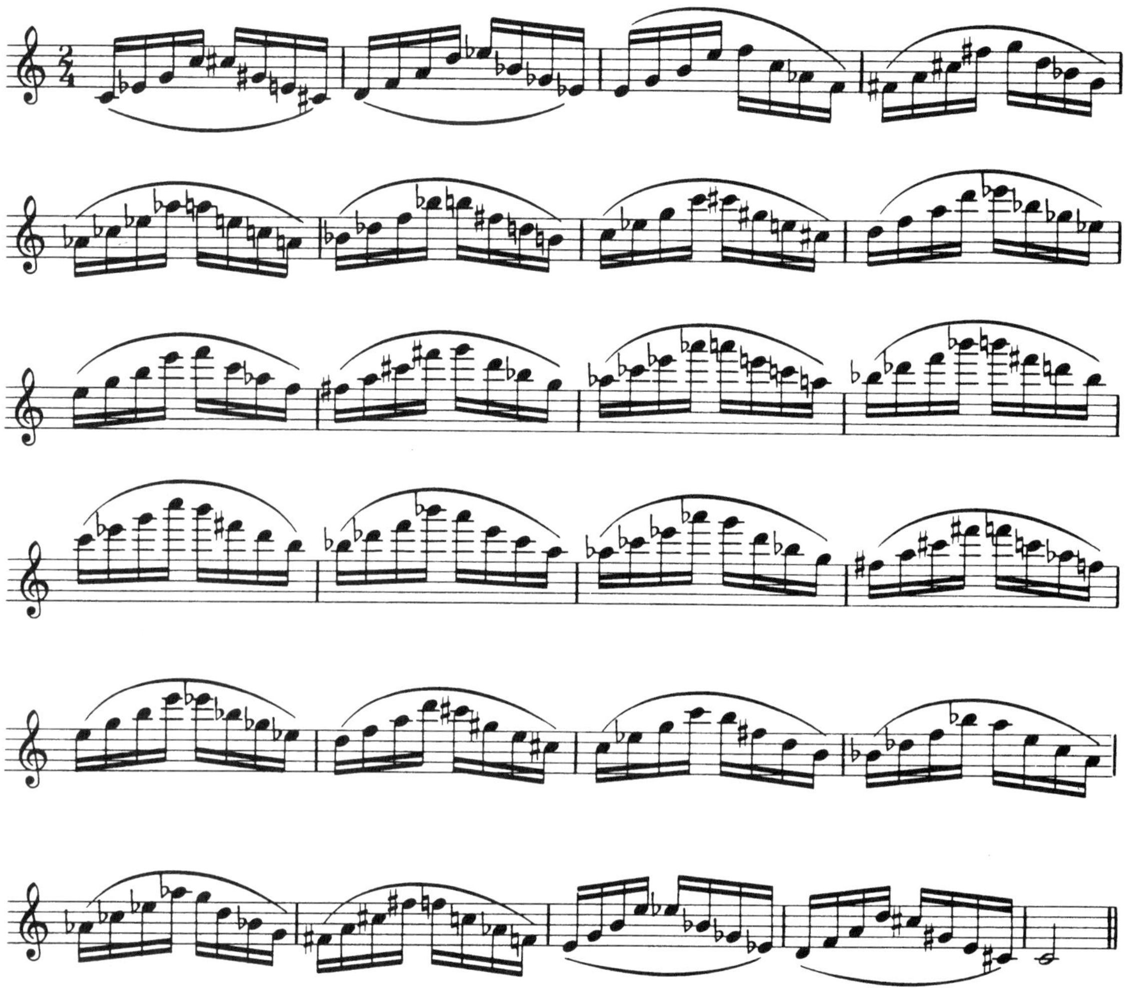

Sequences are like stairs; they can go up and down in sequence or in double sequence. In other words, they can be made to go three steps up and one step down. But, of course, they have to be played fast enough to appreciate the pattern.

etc.

Here are some others. When the rhythm is changed, the possibilities are endless.

DOMINANT SEVENTHS

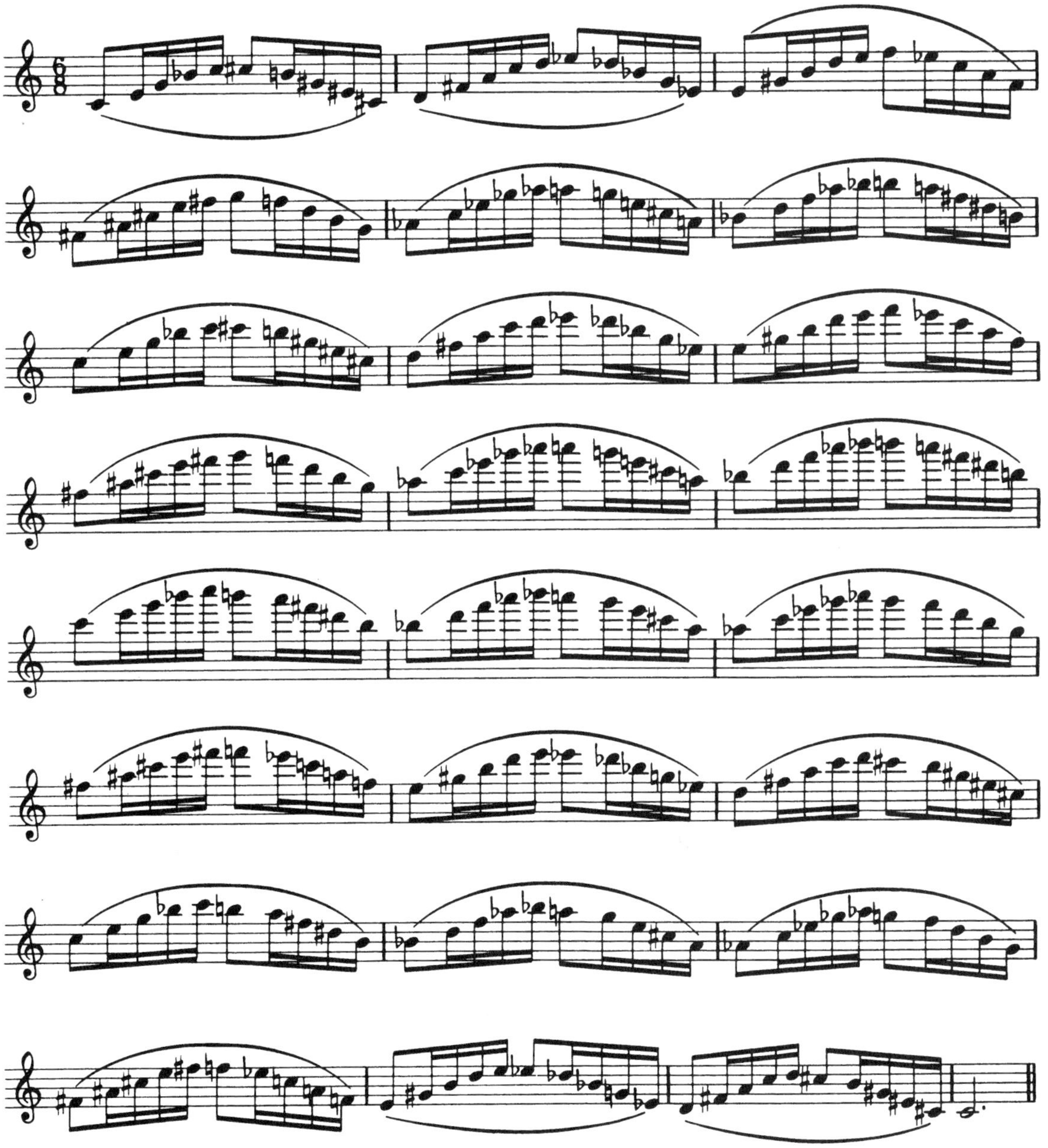

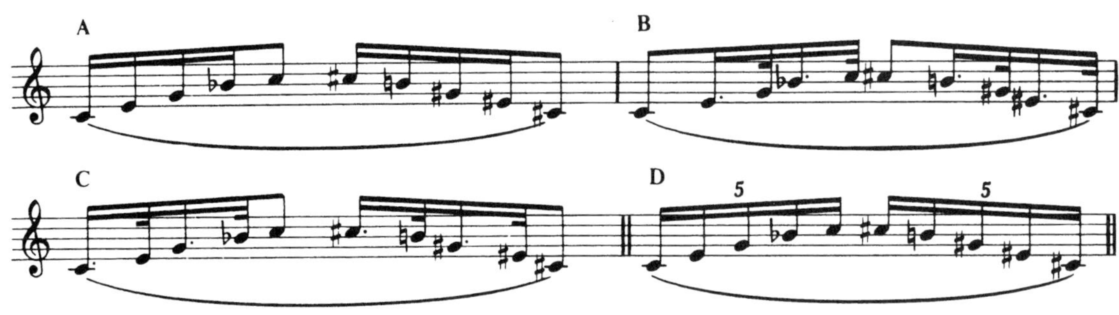

Here are some more ideas or variants:

MAJOR

or perhaps you would prefer a few slinky ones like:

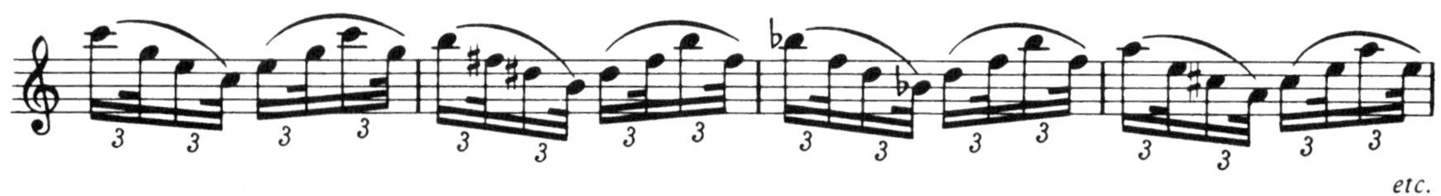

or

DIMINISHED TRIADS

Diminished triads are very beautiful and as there are only three groups of different notes, they are somewhat easier to remember:

and

and

and, of course

and therefore

The scale sequences which follow are not easy but are still a most valuable form of practice:

MAJOR

MINOR

Some examples of the use of sequences can be found at the end of this book.

EXAMPLES

Here are some extracts from the flute repertoire which illustrate the various points raised in this book.

TECHNIQUE

ST JOHN PASSION — J. S. BACH

No. 25

SYMPHONIA DOMESTICA — R. STRAUSS[1]

Scherzo

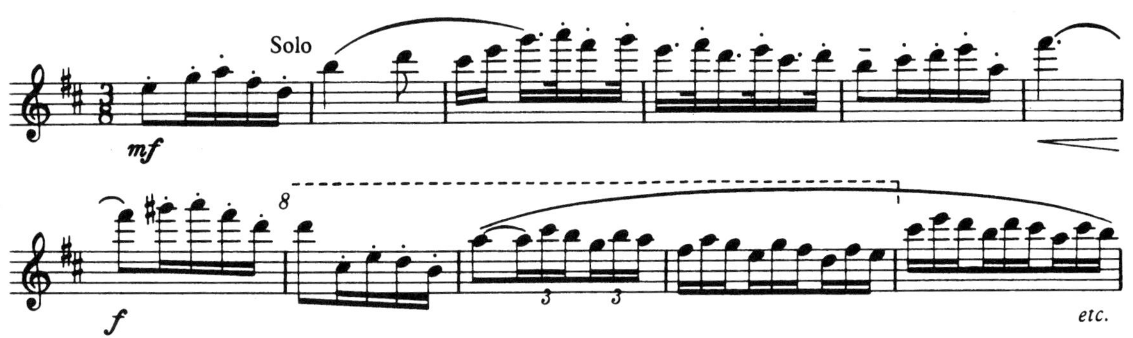

TILL EULENSPIEGEL — R. STRAUSS[2]

TRILLS

SYMPHONY NO. 5 — SHOSTAKOVICH

IL PENSIEROSO — HANDEL

VARIATIONS ON A THEME OF ROSSINI CHOPIN

CHANSON D'AMORE DOPPLER

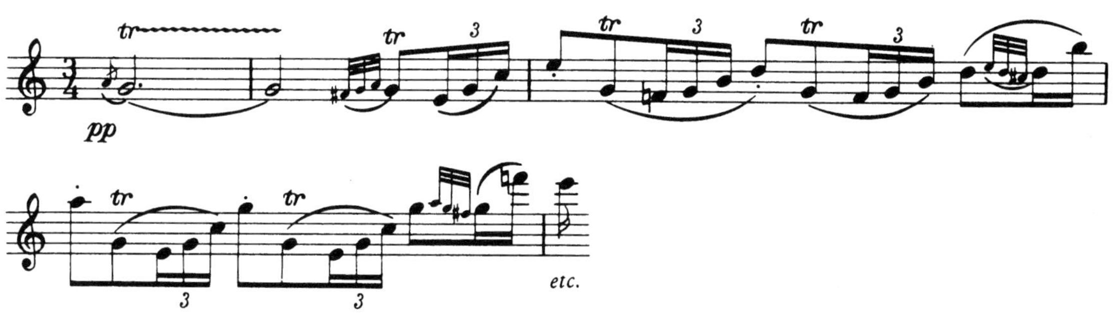

SONATINE DUTILLEUX[3]

SUITE B. GODARD

GODARD: this often causes the young player to stumble at this point:

13th GRAND SOLO TULOU

How grand this ending sounds! The trills add such excitement to the final bars of this solo:

SEQUENCES

CONCERTO IN G C. P. E. BACH

AIRS VALAQUES DOPPLER

FANTASIE PASTORALE HONGROISE

DOPPLER

CANTABILE E PRESTO

ENESCO[4]

PIECE

IBERT[5]

[4]Reproduced by permission of Enoch et Cie—Paris, U.K. and Commonwealth agents Edwin Ashdown Ltd.

TREVOR WYE

OMNIBUS EDITION BOOKS 1-5

PRACTICE BOOKS for the flute

VOLUME 3
Articulation

CONTENTS

ARTICULATION—GENERAL

Articulation is the speech of music. No matter how powerful your musical ideas, they will not be easily communicated to your audience without good articulation. When we talk of someone being articulate, we mean that they are able to express themselves clearly. It's the same in music, though in instrumental learning we usually mean *two* things by the word articulation:

(a) the use in music of slurs and dots.

(b) the use of the tongue.

Both of these meanings will be discussed in this book. In the other two companion books on TONE and TECHNIQUE, you were given exercises to do which had a practical musical and technical value. In this book, because of the way in which our tongues work and the mental problems which arise, you will find exercises which must be practised for their own sake; exercises to try to free the tongue from tramline thinking and exercises which give *you* complete control of your tongue.

More of that later.

Before tackling any of these exercises, consult your teacher on what exercises are best for you at the moment. *This book cannot replace a good teacher.*

ARTICULATION—I

SLURS

Throughout musical history, players have used the slur in a variety of ways and for different reasons. In the eighteenth century, when and when not to slur was largely a question firstly of the common practice of the period and secondly of the technical possibilities of the instrument. Here are a few of the rules: in general, intervals of up to a fifth were slurred when they were part of a *sequence* or *pattern* of notes; for fifths themselves, it was a question of taste as to whether to tongue or slur; intervals larger than a fifth were generally tongued. If in a passage there were recurring patterns of two or three or four notes, then these notes were slurred, for example:

Usage differed in different periods of history.

In the nineteenth century, slurring was often used for 'variety'. Each country, too, had its particular style in the use of slurs.

Without going into any more detail, it *is* important to understand what the slur does on a wind instrument and, more important, what it does for musical language.

A SLUR OVER TWO NOTES RAISES THE IMPORTANCE OF THE FIRST NOTE AND DIMINISHES THE IMPORTANCE OF THE SECOND NOTE.

This principle was largely accepted as having precedence over any conventional rules. There are countless examples of how that rule can be broken but it will, for the moment, suffice as a *basis* for a better understanding of articulation.

Suppose, as a composer, you wrote this group of notes:

in which you might wish to indicate that some notes were more important than others;

then you would place a slur over those notes, like this:

Similarly, using your same nine notes, if you wish to indicate:

then write, and play, the slurs like this:

Here are some other examples:

In a musical phrase, if you decide that the skeleton, or basic tune, consists of *longer* notes that those written, then slurs should be put in accordingly. The harmonic movement should also influence your choice of where to put the slurs. Remember that eighteenth-century composers rarely marked slurs or dots or indeed any nuances. It was left to the good judgement of the performer.
Try working these examples out. Mark in where you think there should be slurs:

Don't put in too many slurs or you will have too many bumps or beats. Your teacher will advise you on what is good taste.

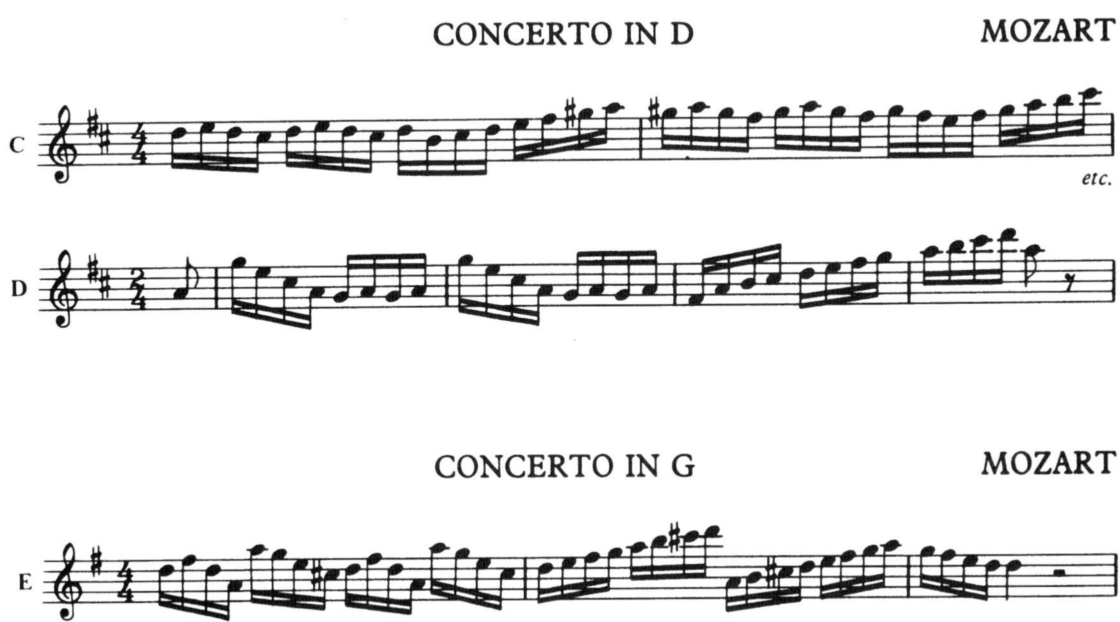

When you have marked in the slurs, then it follows that you must *help* the slurs that you have put in with your performance of them. You are now the editor. Don't argue with your own slurs. Therefore, when playing:

phrase it like this:

similarly this:

is played like this:

Of course, if you feel that all the notes are of *equal* importance, you can tongue all of them. Or slur all of them. It depends on the piece.
Be sure to understand that this rule is only a *basis* on which to build your editorial ideas. There are *many* ways of playing a phrase; for instance, all the notes can be tongued but the first of each group—the skeleton or backbone notes—could be accented or *lengthened* slightly. And again it is important to understand that when all the exercises in this book have been mastered, there are many shades of meaning and difference in each articulation, so that one can tongue all the notes gently but to the audience it can sound *almost* slurred. To a discerning ear, there is a difference. In the palette of articulation there are many colours.
This is what interpretation is partly about. It is not possible to interpret if you are inarticulate!

In this passage:

SONATA IN G MINOR attrib. J. S. BACH

if you feel that the basic tune is:

then slur the notes like this:

If you think this is what Bach meant:

then slur like this:

Play the passage like this:

if you think it should sound like this:

When performing slurs, you must remember that a slur places prominence on the first of a group of slurred notes and puts the rest of the group in the shade. You must also *play* them like that.

It would be foolish to argue with your own or someone else's editorial articulation.

IT WOULD BE MUCH BETTER TO CHANGE IT.

Practise the articulation exercises which follow, and invent some mixed articulations to practise using the same notes. *Do not shorten the last note of a slur.*

In the sections which follow, remember what you have learned and try to apply these simple rules to exercises which contain slurs.

ARTICULATION – II – SINGLE TONGUING*

Articulation is the language of the flute. The study of articulation is vital to good flute playing. Single tonguing is the most important articulation of all. When practising this section on single tonguing, assume that, like the other woodwind instruments, double tonguing doesn't exist. Single tonguing should be practised until very fast; don't be lazy and use double tonguing. Good single tonguing will also help *considerably* towards fluency in double and triple tonguing.

But first, moderate speed single tonguing must have 'bounce'. To obtain this, practise the exercise (a) *using the diaphragm*† *only* to start and stop the note. This muscle must be trained to start and stop quickly therefore, practise the exercise – and all its 24 modulations! – *Loud, Short, and Fast.* For the first few days try to achieve short notes; later speed them up and finally try to play short, fast and loud.

To master this first exercise is to lay the firm foundation of all that is to follow in this book – and more; it trains the muscle to respond quickly in any given movement of the air column i.e. for octave playing, vibrato and supporting the tone. Without the use of the diaphragm your articulation will be *dead.*

Do not proceed until you have made good progress with this exercise** – however long it takes!

When you have worked at this for a time, modulate to D minor:

The articulation problems – clarity, speed and tone – are often different for each key. After D minor, try to play the exercise by ear (or write it out if this is difficult) in the following sequence: B flat major; G minor; E flat major; C minor; A flat major etc., through a total of twenty-four keys.

Single tonguing: work now at (a) *using* your new found diaphragm technique but use the tongue to *start* the note. Tongue forward. Try to obtain a *clear* sound. Aim for a neat clean start. Never *stop* the note with your tongue.

An important point:
Don't try to spend *all* your practice time on one thing, such as articulation. Articulation can take a long time to master. A little time spent on it every day will, like most things, work wonders. It is a question of *time, patience* and *intelligent work.*

* See also PROPER FLUTE PLAYING, p.22, and VOL.6 – ADVANCED PRACTICE, p.26.
† Diaphragm is the term commonly used; in fact the muscles undergoing training here are the abdominal muscles.
** This exercise has already appeared as a tone-colour study in VOL.I – TONE.

Play the first exercise. If you observe the rhythm carefully, you will see that the ratio between the first and second notes is 3:1.
NEVER let it become 2:1 as in *The Teddy Bears' Picnic*.

To sum up:
(a) *don't* use double tonguing in this section—it's cheating!
(b) practise all the exercises both *piano* and *forte*.
(c) strive for a clear tone.
(d) try to increase the speed a little each day.
(e) little and often!
(f) play them in *all* keys, if possible.

After a few days, change the rhythm to double-dotted notes:

The ratio is now 7:1. This is not easy but it is *very* worthwhile.
Do practise the *whole* exercise.
To ensure that tongue and fingers work together, also practise the exercise like this:

and now like this, but keep the rhythm accurate:

To increase the speed of single tonguing further, practise the whole exercise first like this:

As the single tonguing becomes faster, the diaphragm will cease to 'bounce' for every note but will continue to support the tone.

and now like this:

As the tongue becomes stronger, so the muscles can *maintain* single tonguing for longer periods.

Throughout these exercises, and those which follow, practise with a good tone. The quality of sound when articulating is most important.

There is often a difficulty when the notes are so arranged that the tongue is thrown out of gear. This conflict between brain and tongue must be overcome.

Here are some more variations which will help with this problem:

Now to increase the speed further:

If you have had difficulty in gaining some velocity in previous exercises, then try these variations. They are, in any case, good pratice fodder.

Do not shorten the last note of a slur.

Whilst slurring, the tongue is resting, and by gradually removing the slurs the tongue works a little harder and becomes stronger.

Remember: before practising this next section, a good control of single tonguing will save time and will help all other forms of articulation. A lot of time spent on these exercises will be most rewarding.
You must be the master of your tongue, not its servant!

PROBLEMS BOX

1) Exercise 2 is difficult? Then spend more time on it! Many find this and No.4 difficult. Use *single* tonguing – don't be tempted to use double tonguing!

2) Your tongue is in advance of your fingers? Practise VOL. II – TECHNIQUE, and use more of your time on the exercises in that book.

3) The sound is unclear when tonguing? Ask your teacher about this. Try to tongue forward in the mouth and as lightly as possible*. Try not to cause too much disturbance in the mouth by over vigorous use of the tongue. Very often, the *base* of the tongue moves too much and the air passing through the mouth is disturbed. Intelligent practice of these exercises – and some patience – will gradually transfer the muscular movement to the front of the tongue. The result?: a lighter and neat articulation. Think of all the exercises as *tone* exercises instead of just exercises for the tongue.

ARTICULATION – III

DOUBLE TONGUING

Before practising this section the achievement of a good mastery of single tonguing is important.
This exercise and all its variations illustrate a *system of working*. This system can be applied to all articulation exercises and scales. If you are a beginner, your teacher will advise you on the basic movement of the tongue.
Don't expect rapid results. *Regular* practice will soon make the muscles move easily. Practise the basic movement of double tonguing *without* the flute, when walking, sitting on buses, etc. Valuable practice time can thus be saved.
In the exercises, some metronome marks have been put in, but aim to increase the speed every few days. Don't practise double or triple tonguing *slowly*. The 'K' or 'G' should be a reflex. It is better to practise *quickly* in short bursts. Think of these exercises as tone exercises involving the use of the tongue.
Be patient.

This is the first basic exercise which you will need to refer to in the subsequent variations. When you have read through it, start practising Exercise 1. When, and only when, it is fairly easy to play, go on to No. 2 and so on.

* See PROPER FLUTE PLAYING, p.22.

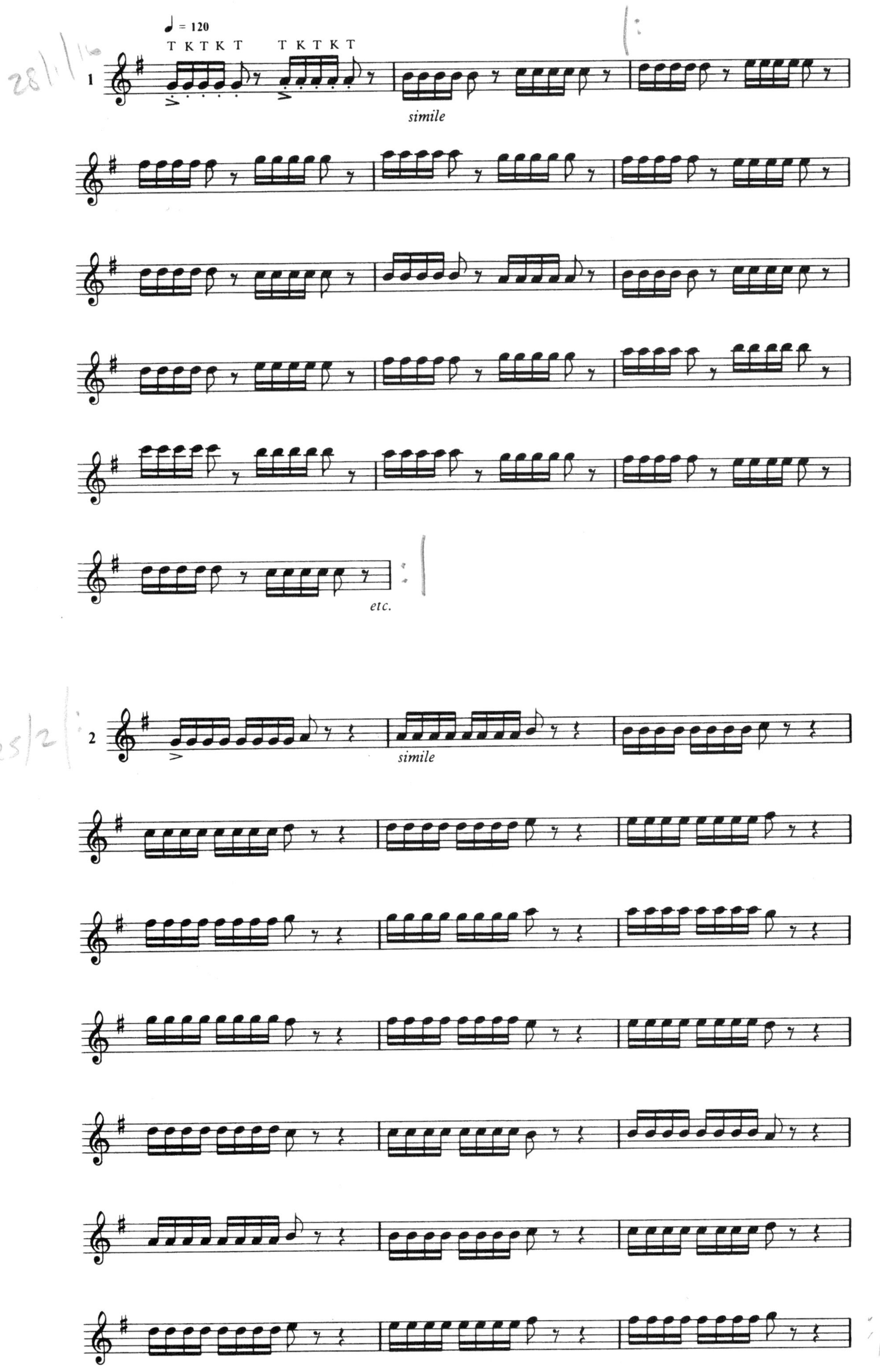

♩ = 120
T K T K T T K T K T
1
simile
etc.
2
simile

etc.

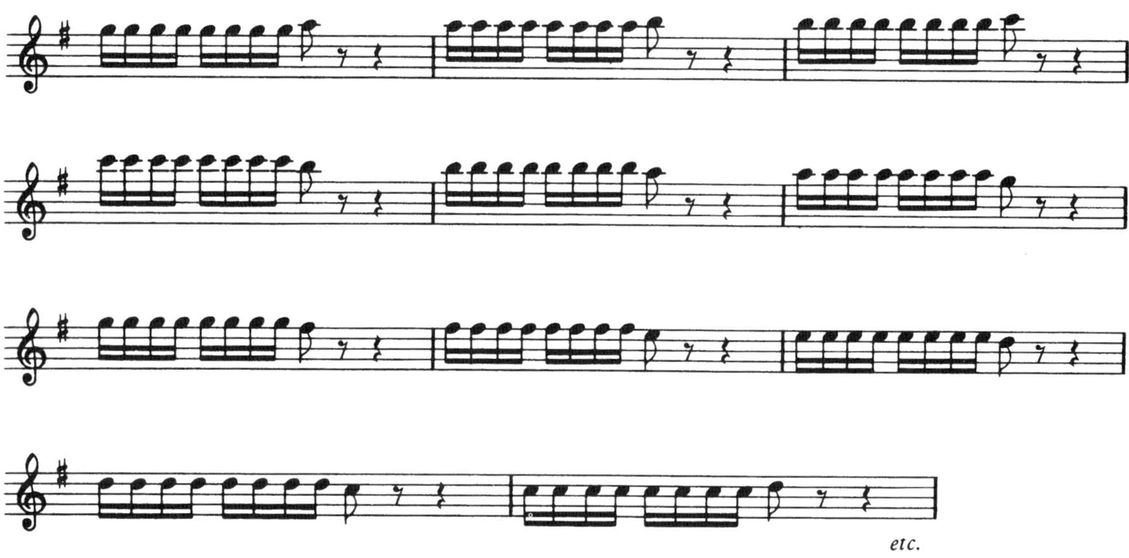

Make the tongue work like clockwork: *precise*, *neat*, *smooth* and *very accurate*.

3

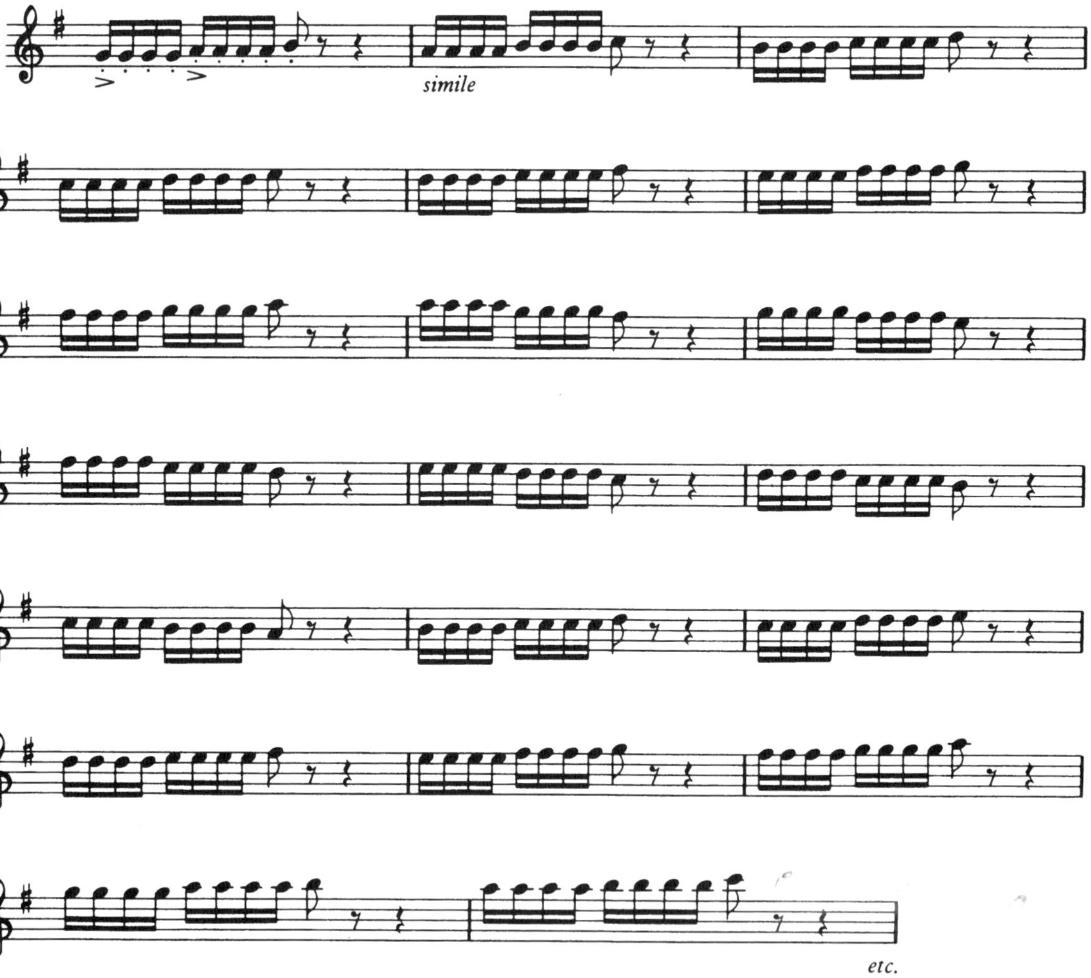
simile
etc.

4

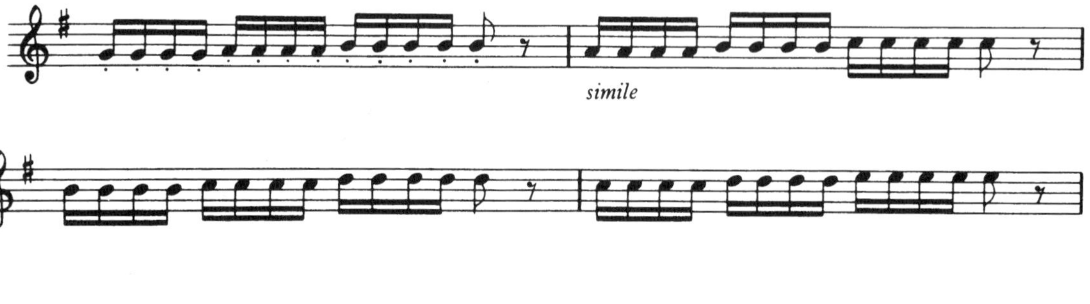
simile

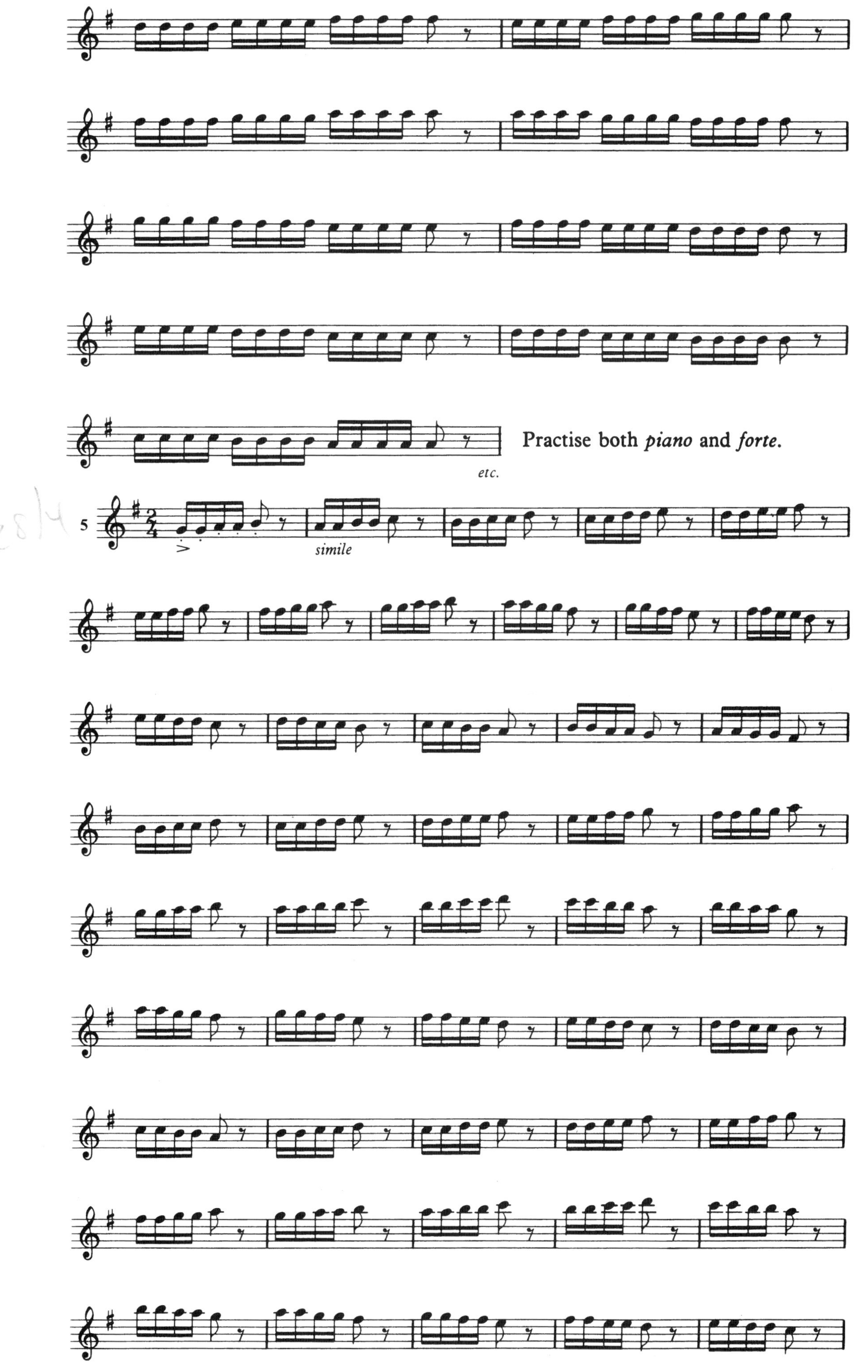
Practise both *piano* and *forte*.
etc.
5
simile

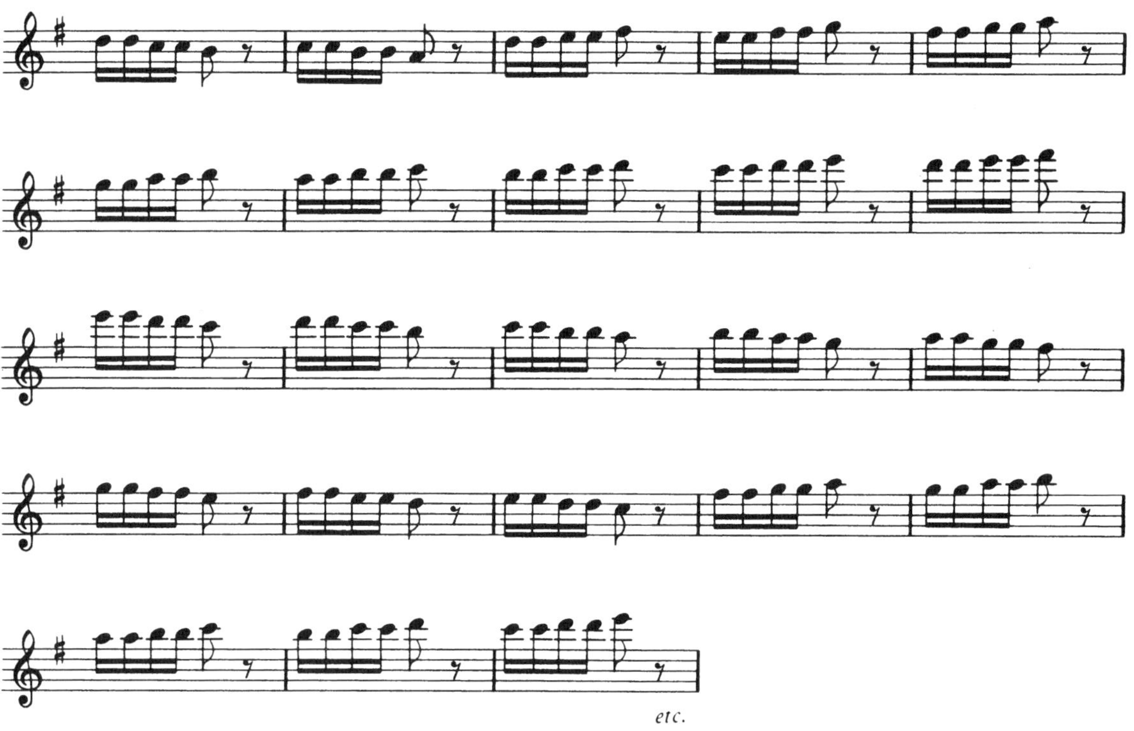

Don't practise double tonguing slowly; it has little value. The back stroke or rebound of the tongue is like a reflex action and slow practice is akin to learning to run slowly or jump in the air in slow motion; not much use!

6

etc.

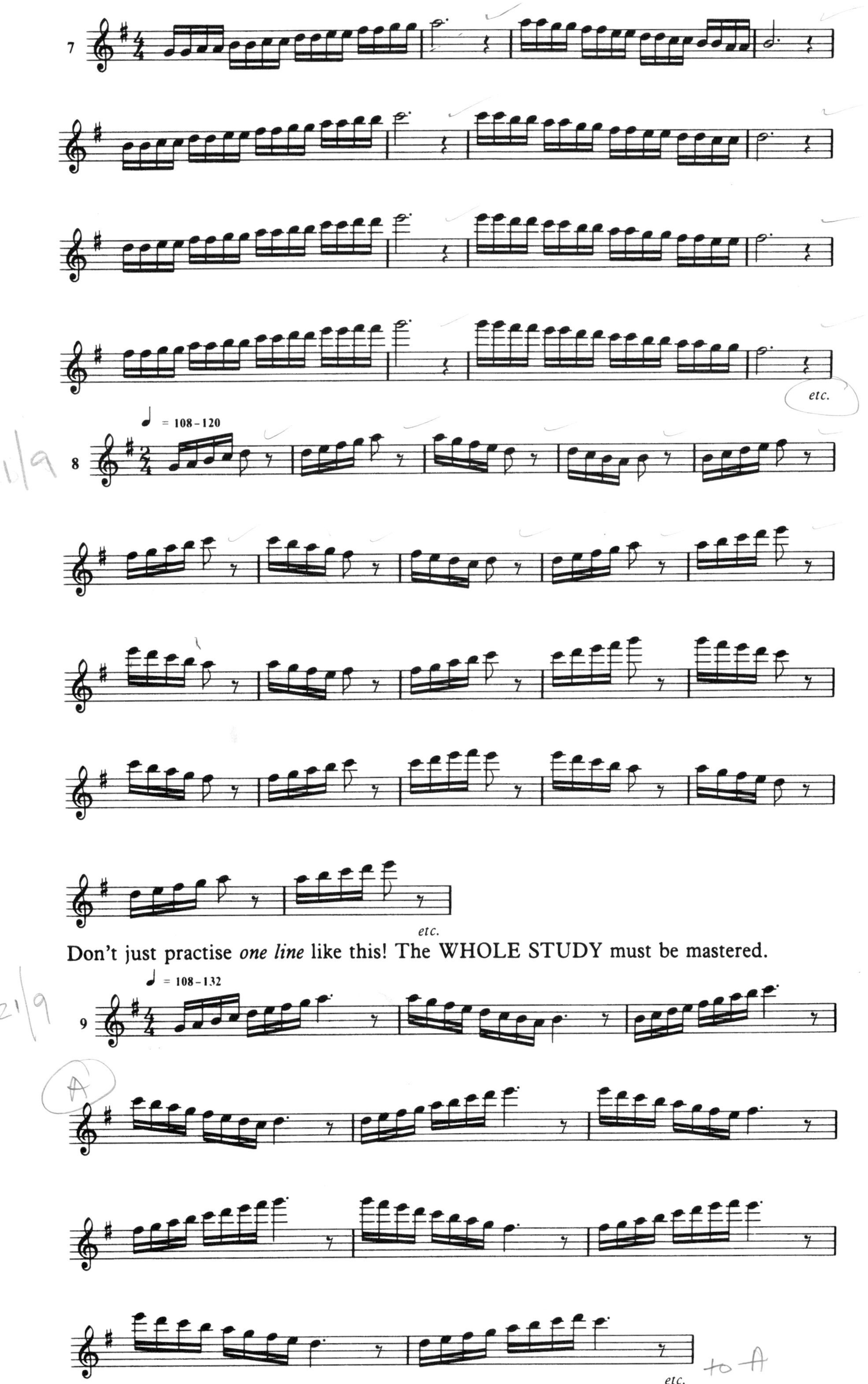

Don't just practise *one line* like this! The WHOLE STUDY must be mastered.

As in the single tonguing exercises, slurs can be used to give the tongue a short rest. Don't go on to No. 12 until No. 11 is very fluent.

Do not shorten the last note of a slur.

In the next two exercises, you are doing battle with your own brain. Your reflexes take over and try to make your tongue work only in a prescribed way.

Have you practised these studies both *piano* and *forte*?

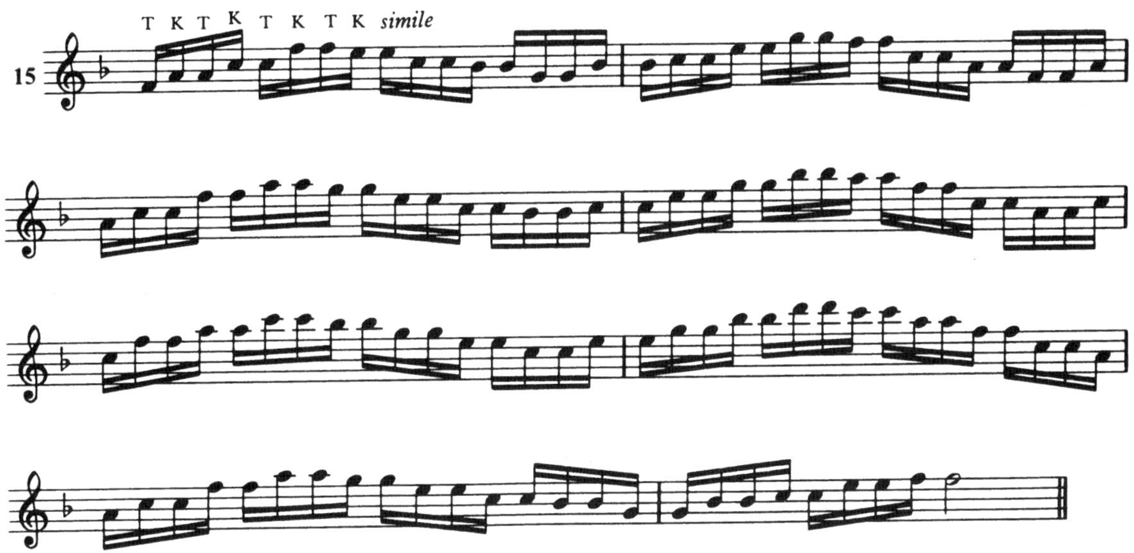

Try to make your tongue go as fast as possible, but do remember to play with a good tone.

Play the exercises in other keys; you will find that each key has its own special articulation difficulties.
As in the single tonguing section, practise the exercises in a sequence:

through twenty-four keys in all.

Finally, if for any reason the exercises become boring, or you just don't happen to like them, apply the *principle* of this method of practice to any study, or even to an orchestral passage.

PROBLEMS BOX

1) You can't get your tongue to move fast enough? Practise—without the flute—on buses, or when walking. Don't use the flute as a piece of gymnastic apparatus. Tongue forward in the mouth—near the teeth. As the weeks go by, the base of the tongue—which is creating such an upheaval in the mouth—will move less and less and most of the action will be in the tip of the tongue. Your articulation will then sound clearer.

2) Your tongue gets tired? That's quite normal. Exercise it every day both with and without the flute.
When the tongue gets *really* tired, have a legato exercise on the music-stand to practise for a few moments to provide a rest for the muscles—then continue tonguing.

3) Your articulation limps with the 'K' weaker than the 'T' like this?:

That too, is a common problem. Starting off with the back stroke ('K') play the double tonguing exercise all through. Also practise *saying* it, starting with 'K'. Put *accents* on all 'Ks'. It will help to get rid of the unevenness.

These exercises have no musical value, but they are very important if you wish to have complete freedom of articulation both in your muscles and in your mind. And, more important, they are most beneficial in securing *co-ordination* between the fingers and tongue.

4) If after much practice the *tone* in your articulation is not CLEAR, try 'bending' notes whilst tonguing. See the section on Pitch Control in VOL. I—TONE.

BE PATIENT: PRACTISE ARTICULATION EVERY DAY.

ARTICULATION—IV

TRIPLE TONGUING

By now, you will have become accustomed to the manner of practising articulation and will be familiar with the pattern of exercises which follow.
First, our basic exercise:

(after Reichert)

which is followed by a series of variations.

Don't go on until the previous exercise has been mastered. Observe, too, the following points:

(a) practise without the flute; the basic tongue movement must be mastered by itself.
(b) tongue forward in the mouth; try to be neat and precise.
(c) practise these exercises as *tone* exercises.
(d) practise both piano *and* forte.
(e) try to increase the speed a little every day.
(f) practise triple tonguing little and often!

3

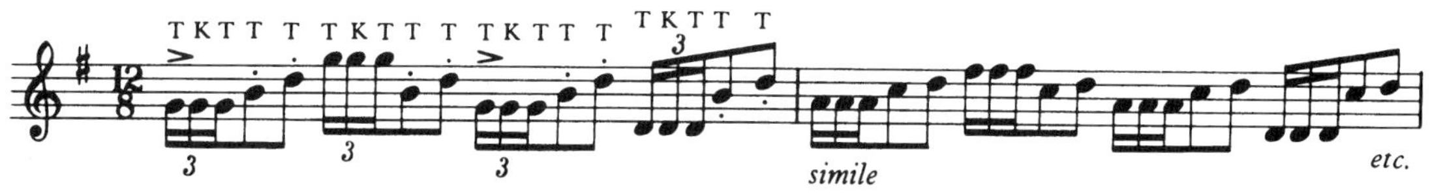

4

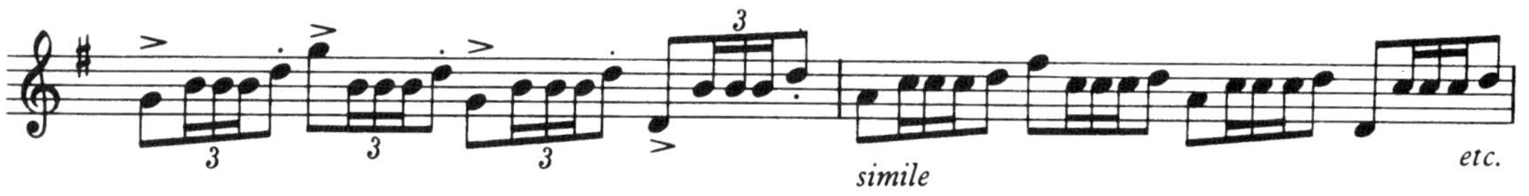

5

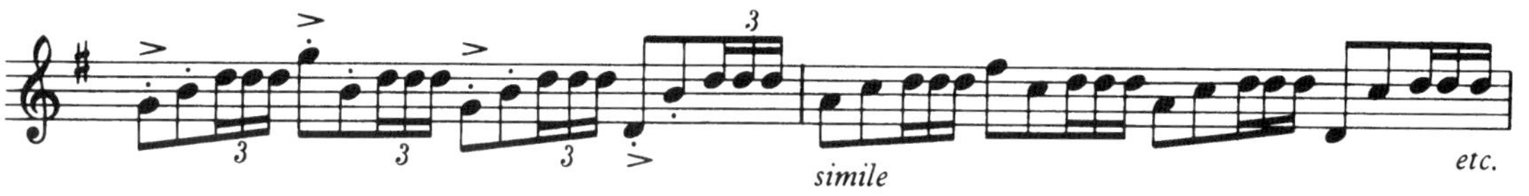

6

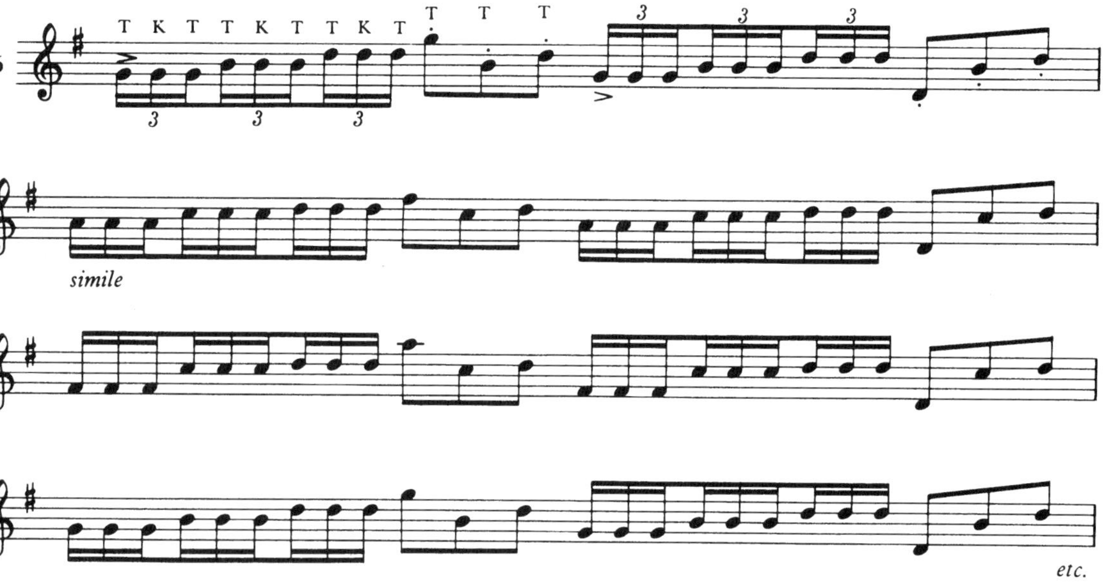

Don't go on until you feel you could play No. 6 in public!

7

8

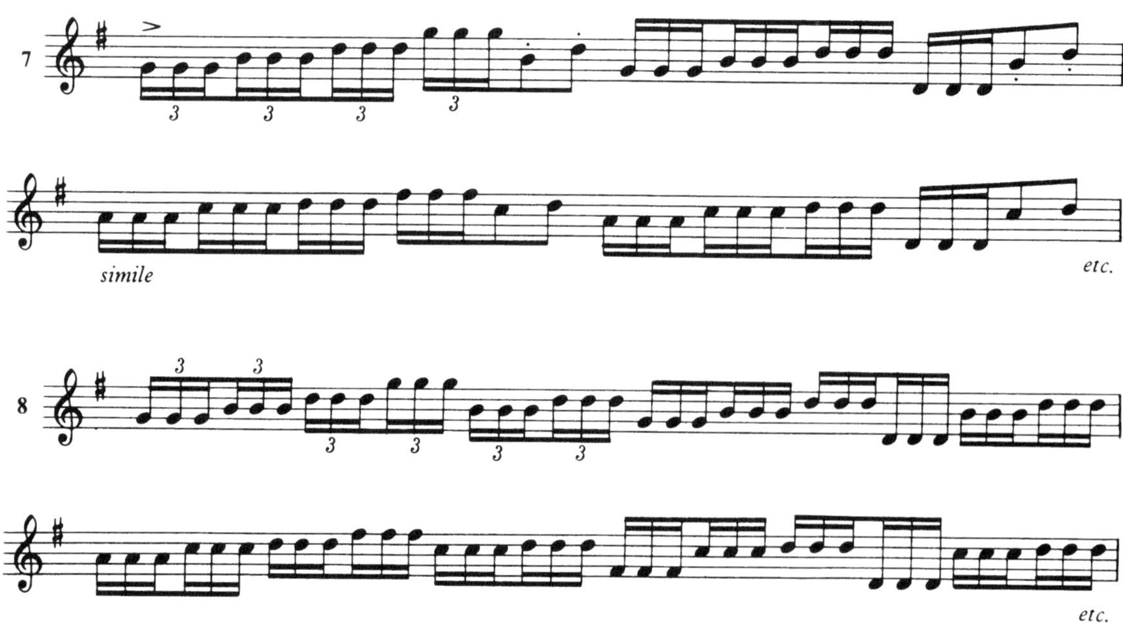

Practise the exercises ALL THROUGH, not just a few bars.

This next one for a bit of fun:

In order to obtain complete freedom of your tongue and your unconscious reflexes, it would be wise to practise the exercises like this:

When you tackle these, you will understand the problem!

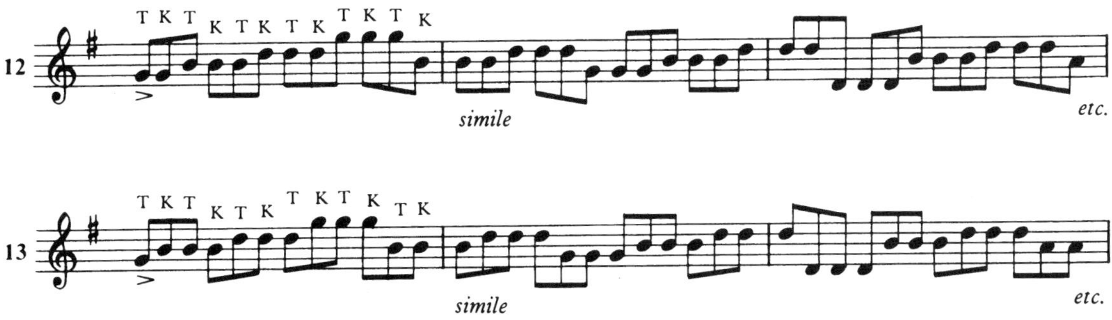

The exercises above are only an outline of a method of many, many months of careful practice, and the principle should be applied to all kinds of studies.

Some examples of double and triple tonguing will be found at the end of this book.

GOOD ARTICULATION TAKES A LONG WHILE TO ESTABLISH: REGULAR PRACTICE IS THE REAL ANSWER!

ARTICULATION—V

THE E FLAT PROBLEM

Keeping the first finger of the left hand down for E flat is quite a common fault.* Curiously enough, when the tone is weak, the 'grunt' that is heard at the start of a badly played E flat is less noticeable. As your tone becomes more focussed, so does the 'grunt'! The better player you become, the worse it sounds!
To start with, play Exercise 1 *with* the first finger down for E flat. Play it loud and short; you should soon hear how unpleasant it is. Now repeat, fingering the E flat correctly.

Do the same in Exercise 2, but this time keep the first finger down for both *E flat and D.* Tongue short and loud.

Now try Exercise 3, fingering as in Exercise 2, but finger the C as you would for *low* C. Notice how the 'grunt' gets progressively worse.

Do the same with Exercise 4. The 'grunt' is distinctly worse in tongued passages than in slurred ones. Play it both slurred and staccato.

Play these four exercises *wrongly* each day for a week before practising the three E flat exercises which follow. In this way you will soon learn to *hear* the difference which will help you recognise the 'grunt' when it occurs in other exercises and pieces. It is, after all, our ears which are offended by the wrong fingering.

*The most frequently recurring fault found in young players. Theobald Boehm, who designed our flute, also designed E flat and D to be played with the first finger raised. *Top* E flat should, of course, be played with *all* fingers down.

THREE E FLAT EXERCISES

These are especially for E flats. Use the first finger right hand for B flat.* When you can play it through without mistakes, you are really making progress. Play both legato and staccato.

T.W.

Play this next exercise twice through. If you should play even *one* bad E flat—or a D natural with the 1st finger on—then go back and repeat. Continue repeating until faultless. Then try four times through without a mistake. Eight times through and you have done well. *No cheating!*

T.W.

Exercise 3.

Besides concentrating on ensuring that the first finger is *off* for E flat, *be sure* also to use the D sharp key for *all* notes except D natural. You will really have to concentrate in this study.

*See VOL. II—TECHNIQUE.

T.W.

NERVES*

Everyone suffers—and benefits—from nerves. A performer who is never nervous is a very rare animal indeed. Nerves are essential to performance, though that is, I know, hard to believe when your knees are trembling, fingers shaking, stomach queasy, mouth dry and a sweat breaks out!

'Nerves' are the effects felt by substances called adrenalin and acetylcholine on the nerves of our bodies. Adrenalin and acetylcholine and other substances with long names are released by glands in the body in response to orders from the brain. The purpose of adrenalin is to give a quicker and more positive response to danger. When man, armed only with a club, was faced by a brontosaurus, adrenalin was released in his body which

*This section was read and approved by David Mendel F.R.C.P., Consultant, St Thomas's Hospital, London.

gave his muscles a supercharger to fight harder, or to run away faster. Without a fight—or a run—adrenalin irritates. Adrenalin is nevertheless, as all musicians and actors will tell you, important to public performance. It helps us to play better. Unfortunately, our bodies often give us more than is necessary. This extra quantity is what concerns us here because it is adrenalin which causes your mouth to dry up, your knees to tremble, etc., and acetylcholine which, the opposite to adrenalin, causes you to go pale, lowers your blood pressure, makes you feel faint, etc.

What starts it all? Nerves are triggered off by (a) *conscious fear*, or (b) *a subconscious loop*. It is not going to be easy to discover which of these two causes *your* particular anxiety. *Conscious fear* can be helped in a number of ways, notably by finding out what causes the fear.

1) Fear of the audience: when first appearing on the platform *look at your audience*. There is not a brontosaurus amongst them! Talk to them, announce your pieces, tell stories about them. All this will help to reduce the fear, though it may take time.

2) Learn the music well: do not publicly perform pieces beyond your ability. Learn the difficult bits from memory. If and when a moment of panic does come, an automatic pilot takes over *if* the music has been well mastered.

A subconscious loop is a recurring fear triggered off by the subconscious part of your memory *whether or not there is anything to be afraid of*. For example: you have had three or four unpleasant visits to the headmaster/headmistress. On being informed that your presence is required, though this time it is to be congratulated for some school event, once again adrenalin starts to flow and you feel fear. You have a partial loop: headmaster=fear=adrenalin. Unfortunately we have a tendency to worry about *being afraid* and its subsequent effect on the performance. Knowing that we are going to experience fear, adrenalin is released which gives even more grounds for anxiety. Then we have a real loop: concert=anxiety=adrenalin=anxiety about fear=more adrenalin etc, etc, etc. It is possible to break a loop by the method described above in 1) and 2). Do try this first. This too may help: the population is largely divided into two groups who, when anxious, are dominated by either adrenalin or acetylcholine. There are, of course, all the shades in between. To find out which group you belong to, either (a) allow boiled sweets—such as barley sugar—to dissolve slowly in the mouth during the day of the concert, to maintain the blood-sugar level which may have dropped due to your anxiety, or (b) take a sea sickness pill of the kind readily available over the counter at a chemist's shop. Don't take both together. Try them out separately on less important occasions to see which one seems to help you the most. Don't forget to try 1 and 2 above first, and remember that *some* nervousness makes for a better performance. If after some experiments you are still very nervous, an alcoholic drink before the concert can be most beneficial. I hesitate to recommend this step for fear (?) of being misunderstood. A small amount of alcohol before a concert can work wonders. It may be the scissors to break the loop. Contrary to popular belief, when strong anxiety or excitement is felt, very little alcohol is absorbed by the stomach, so that you are most unlikely to get drunk!
Having trodden thus far on this thorny path, advanced students may like to know that there are now drugs which can help nerves and should seriously be considered for important occasions. Experiments with students from the London music colleges have shown most promising results. These drugs, known as beta-blockers, restrict the effect of adrenalin on the body with little or no side-effects. They are available only on prescription from a doctor. Like earlier suggestions, they should first be tried on less important occasions so that you can judge your response to them.

Readers who may have some misgivings about the use of alcohol or drugs may care to reflect on the effect of nerves and strain on the body which can cause a great deal of damage over a period of time. For the more advanced student or professional player who is competing in an international competition or an important audition, or who is giving a concert debut, for them this event is the culmination of many years of study and achievement. An attack of nerves at this stage could be all important and decisive.

You should read the section on relaxation in VOL. II—TECHNIQUE. It may also prove helpful.

DOUBLE TONGUING

CONCERTO IN D MINOR — C. P. E. BACH

CANTABILE E PRESTO — ENESCO[1]

CLOCK SYMPHONY — HAYDN

TRIPLE TONGUING

ITALIAN SYMPHONY — MENDELSSOHN

SONATE EN CONCERT — J-M. DAMASE[2]

TREVOR WYE

OMNIBUS EDITION BOOKS 1-5

PRACTICE BOOKS for the *flute*

VOLUME 4

Intonation and Vibrato

CONTENTS

FOREWORD

This Practice Book is concerned with everything which affects or relates to playing in tune.* It may, in places, confuse you. Don't worry. In time, all will be clear.
Reading through this book will not give you the instant ability to play in tune. Play the exercises in each section carefully and often. The acquisition of an 'ear' does not come easily, and, when once obtained, needs constant refreshment.
Without practice, the ability to hear very small changes in pitch and to discern faults in intervals can soon be lost. The ear becomes 'blunt' if not put to work often, as any piano tuner will confirm. To get the most out of this book you will need a few basic tools: a tuning fork, access to a well-tuned piano, some basic adjusting tools for your flute, but, most important of all, time, patience and intelligent work!

The growth in small electronic tuning machines has made easy the whole process of learning to play in tune and checking your instrument.

If it isn't possible to buy one, then borrow one for a few days. What it can tell you, especially about the third octave, may be surprising.

*The exercises for achieving this can be found in VOL.I - TONE pp.34-6 and in PROPER FLUTE PLAYING pp.20-1.

THE CHORD OF NATURE

For this first experiment you will need a piano which is well in tune. It is not important, at this stage, if the piano is totally above or below pitch though it *must* be in tune with itself. First, open the lid wide. If it is an upright piano remove the top front. The fasteners for this can be found just inside the top lid on the left and right. Find a bass note on the piano which is rich, vibrant and in tune – some notes have two or three strings each – it is important that the note has no sourness. Play the note forte and see if you can hear more than one note sounding softly above your chosen note. With practice, you will soon hear eight or ten different notes sounding together above your chosen bass note. To help you hear these notes more easily, play the bass note (in the example, it is F) with one hand, with the other strike the octave above, briefly:

You should hear the octave sounding together with the bass note. The short note doesn't *make* the upper note sound; it simply draws your attention to the note you should listen for.
Now continue with the exercise below. Allow about ten seconds for each held bass note as some of the upper notes become apparent only after a few seconds have elapsed.

Do not use the pedal.

By now you will have heard most, if not all, of the upper notes. These are called *harmonics* or *overtones* and have a definite relationship to the bass note or *fundamental.* If you have some difficulty in hearing any of these notes, move the position of your head a little.

Now for another experiment; after listening to all the harmonics, hold down the sustaining pedal, and sound your low note again. You will clearly hear all the harmonics sounding as a rich chord, rather like an organ:

For the next experiment, without holding down the sustaining pedal, you must push down the key for each of the short notes, or harmonics, in turn *without the hammer hitting the string and causing the note to sound*, and strike your bass note again loudly. After about one second, release the bass note. Listen.

Repeat for all eight notes separately. Taking the damper off the upper note allows it to sound in sympathy with the harmonics of the bass note. This is called Sympathetic Vibration. Some sympathetic notes sound rather louder than others.
To experience more sympathetic vibration, hold down the sustaining pedal and sing a note loudly into the piano.
Now try different vowel sounds: *Oooh, Aaah, Eeeh etc. Notice that the piano 'plays back' the original sound. This is because each vowel sound has a different mixture of harmonics.*
REMEMBER THAT THE HARMONICS *NEVER CHANGE THEIR SEQUENCE*: what makes the sounds alter is the relative strength of each of the harmonics in the vowel sound. The understanding of this fact is important to any study of tone or intonation because the fundamental tone of all musical instruments is exactly alike; the reason why we hear differences between say, a flute and an oboe is primarily because the flute has few harmonics sounding with any note (about five) and an oboe has many (about thirteen)*.
Why do we hear a difference between two different flute players? Because the sound each player makes – though playing the *same* notes with the *same* harmonics – contains different *quantities* of each harmonic. If flour is the basic ingredient of a cake, then varying the quantity of fruit, eggs, sugar and butter will produce different cakes, though the ingredients remain the same.
Try the piano experiment with a different piano and you will have less difficulty in hearing some harmonics and more difficulty in hearing others, especially the seventh harmonic. Piano makers deliberately try to suppress the seventh harmonic because it sounds so out of tune with the natural note on the piano:

Once again play your bass note: 

Fix your ear, after a few seconds, on to the seventh harmonic. Now softly play the minor seventh on the piano:

There is a slight but discernible difference in intonation. Which is right? They both are! The natural note has been tuned (or adjusted) to conform with Equal Temperament without which it would be impossible to play in all keys. More of this later in the section headed SCALES.

*The starting transient is the scientific term to describe the first fraction of a second of a note and is the other determining factor which helps us recognise different musical sounds.

Here is a list of the Harmonic Series up to the eighth harmonic. There are, of course, many more beyond the first eight, but this list will serve us for now.

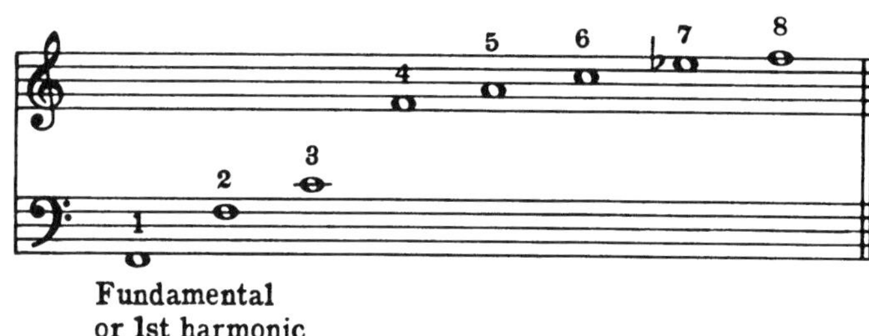

Another harmonic which does not agree with Equal Temperament to which your piano is tuned is the fifth harmonic (A, if you are using F as your bass note). When your bass note has been sounded, the fifth harmonic (which gives, in effect, a major third) rings out loud and clear. What, then, if you wish to play the chord of F minor using your bass F as the root of this chord? A♭ is going to clash badly with the fifth harmonic which is A♮. Play the chord of F major, later adding an A♭ softly at the pitch of the fifth harmonic. *Ouch!* So thought the ancient musicians who decided that any minor chord which has to be sustained for any length became painful, and was better changed to a major chord – especially at the end of a piece – so as to avoid the minor third clashing with the fifth harmonic. This effect is otherwise known as the TIERCE DE PICARDIE.
Do all minor chords have to be changed to major chords? No, they just have to be better in tune to sound right, though if you now play alternate major and minor chords on the piano, you will hear a clarity about the major chord and a bit of *ouch!* in the minor. The scoring of the chord is important, of course, and a well-scored chord can sound 'cleaner'. The pitch of any note can also be changed very slightly on the piano by playing each note with a different nuance: loud=sharper; soft=flatter. A dominant seventh chord will sound better when the seventh is played softly.
Although no flute playing has taken place yet – don't worry! A clear understanding of what has gone before and what is to follow is vital to any future intonation practice.

SCALES

No, not the sort you have to practise to acquire a technique, but the division of the octave into notes and intervals. Music making came first: constructing scales came later to meet the needs of music. In the earliest European music, the need to change key often, as we do today, was not required by composers or listeners. Chord changes were simple. Music was based on the intervals in the Chord of Nature, or the natural Harmonic Series, which means that the notes of the scale match the Harmonic Series you have heard. Unfortunately, the distance between each semitone is not the same. The octave is divided into twelve slightly unequal parts. The notes in this scale when played as chords are pleasing to the ear but if any note of this scale is used as the tonic of a *new* scale, the notes in the new key wouldn't correspond with the notes of the old key. In other words, as the music changed into more remote keys, it would sound less and less pleasing.
If one wants to modulate into other keys, the best compromise is to divide the octave into twelve equal parts, the Equal Tempered Scale.
Here is a diagram which shows the difference between an Equal Tempered Scale and Just Scale or a scale according to the harmonic series.

EQUAL TEMPERED SCALE

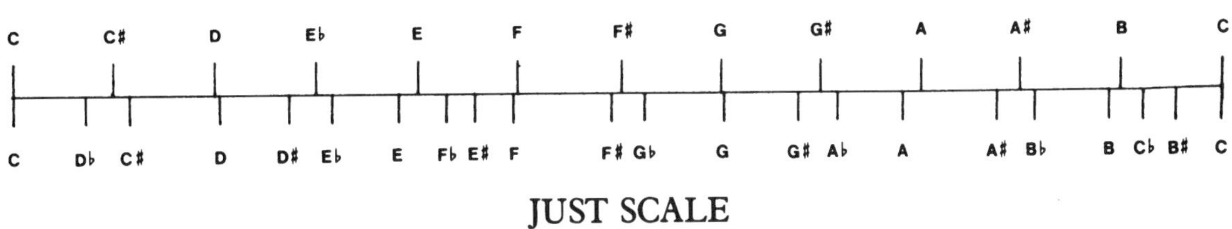

JUST SCALE

Take a ruler and imagine O as C♮, 1 cm as C♯, 2 cms as D, 3 cms as E♭, 4 cms as E♮ etc. The interval C-E, a major third, would appear on the *Just Scale* as about 3¾ cms. Suppose we wanted to use the E (3¾ cms) as the *starting point* to measure another interval. The measurements would not coincide with the remaining measured marks. To change key from C Major to E Major would mean using 3¾ cms as the starting point. To put it another way, imagine a ruler exactly 12 cms long on which the distance between each centimetre varied!
The only sensible solution to our dilemma is to divide the ruler into exactly equal parts, then any point on the ruler can be used as a new starting point.
The same with the octave: divided into twelve equal parts gives Equal Temperament.

The advantages of Equal Temperament are:
1) Changing key, even to remote keys, would sound pleasing on any instrument.
2) All instruments will match each other in scale.

The disadvantage is that: there is a small but discernible 'out of tuneness' in some intervals particularly major and minor thirds.
Look as the diagram again. On the Just Scale there is a difference between F♯ and G♭. Though these are not shown on the diagram, there are also different positions for both double sharps and double flats. To play on a flute constructed to a Just Scale and be able freely to change key, you would need thirty-five notes to one octave and a lot more fingers and arms to play it! As it is, without double sharps and flats, there are twenty notes as compared with twelve notes in the Equal Temperament scale.

In other sections in this book, you will be making experiments to allow you to *hear* these Just Intonation intervals and to appreciate them, though it is not the purpose here to return to the past. Equal Temperament is most certainly here to stay. We have all had our ears trained to hear Equal Temperament as IN TUNE when, in fact, it isn't! One writer referred to it as the Equal T*a*mpered Scale.

If everyone were to play exactly in tune with Equal Temperament however, it would sound very pleasing to the ear, or, acceptably out of tune!
When you have fully understood the next section, you will have a clear idea in which direction to move when you are out of tune with another instrument. Playing in tune will follow.
It is a question of a 'good ear' plus ...., ..., and ....!

FLUTE HARMONICS

Now take up your flute and play low C, overblowing it until it plays the octave above. (The same exercise as in Volume 1 – Tone – pp. 6 and 37).

2nd harmonic

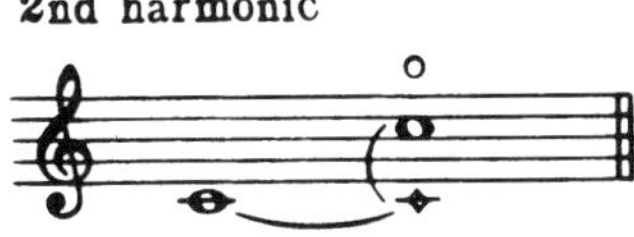

The octaves *should* be in tune (but see the section headed THE FLUTE SCALE).

Now overblow C until it produces G.

Quickly compare the pitch with the natural G fingering.

There is a change in quality – ignore this. Listen only to the pitch. There should only be a very slight difference.
Overblow now to the fourth and on to the fifth harmonic – E above the stave. Compare the pitch of the harmonic E with your natural E fingering. You will notice a large difference: the *harmonic* E is considerably flatter and will correspond in pitch with the E♮ in the diagram of the two Temperaments. Continue the series – if you can – to the sixth harmonic – G – and on to the seventh. When comparing this B♭ with the usual fingering, it seems to be neither B♭ nor A, but somewhere in between. It corresponds with A♯ in the diagram on the Just Scale.

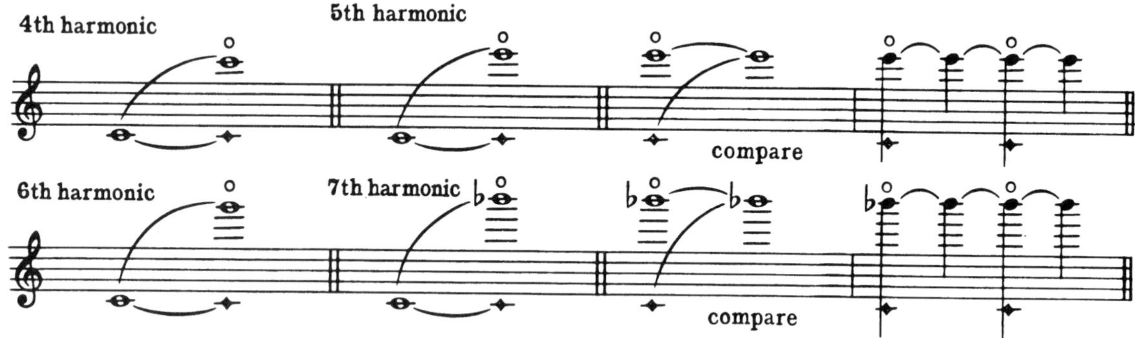

Having observed these differences in pitch between the harmonics and the Equal Tempered tuning on your flute, where does this lead us? Musical scales are made in the process of trying to make music.

It will be obvious that to play in *all* keys at pleasure, the distance between each semitone *must* be the same. This idea of dividing the octave into twelve equal parts is not new, it was first put forward by the Chinese about five thousand years ago and more recently championed by many composers of the eighteenth century including J. S. Bach.

To repeat once more: Equal Temperament means having exactly the same distance between semitones and that, in turn, means division of the octave into twelve equal semitones.

Look at the table below: for simplicity, you will see listed the C Major scale but including an E♭ so that you can compare the C Major and C Minor scales.

A semitone can be divided up into one hundred parts and each part called a cent. There are twelve hundred cents to the octave. In the left hand column are the diatonic intervals from C. Next, are the same notes in cents. The next column contains the intervals in a Just Scale, also divided into cents.

The adjustments which you might wish to make to play *really* in tune are shown in the right hand column headed *Result.* I have measured the amount of sharpness or flatness in pitch required in 'OGGS'. OGGS are anything. I invented them. If you are playing from C to E, then flatten the E by seven oggs, or, quite a bit! The interval C-G is very slightly sharper than in equal temperament.

NOTE	EQUAL TEMPERAMENT (in Cents)	JUST TEMPERAMENT (in Cents)	RESULT THE DIFFERENCE (in Oggs)
C	0	0	0
D	200	204	+2
E♭	300	316	+8
E	400	386	−7
F	500	498	−1
G	700	702	+1
A	900	884	−8
B	1100	1088	−6
C	1200	1200	0

If you really want to sound in tune, you will constantly have to adjust your intonation, depending
(a) on which key your are in, and
(b) on the other instruments playing with you.

I must repeat once again:
THIS BOOK DOES NOT SET OUT TO SUGGEST THAT YOU MUST PLAY ACCORDING TO A JUST TEMPERAMENT SCALE. WHAT YOU LEARN FROM IT IS THAT IF YOU HAVE THE E♮ IN THE CHORD OF C MAJOR IT WILL SOUND *ACCEPTABLE* IF IT IS IN ACCORDANCE WITH EQUAL TEMPERAMENT. IT WILL BE UNACCEPTABLY OUT OF TUNE IF IT IS *SHARPER* THAN EQUAL TEMPERAMENT. IT WILL SOUND PERFECTLY IN TUNE (PROVIDED ALL THE OTHER INSTRUMENTS ARE IN TUNE) IF IT IS FLATTENED BY 7 OGGS *BELOW* EQUAL TEMPERAMENT.

The chart needs now to be translated into intervals in all keys rather than just in C Major and the adjustment you might wish to make committed to memory:

INTERVAL	*ADJUSTMENT IN OGGS*
MAJOR SECOND	+2
MINOR THIRD	+8
MAJOR THIRD	−7
PERFECT FOURTH	−1
PERFECT FIFTH	+1
MAJOR SIXTH	−8
MAJOR SEVENTH	−6

Notice that if the interval of a perfect fifth has to be made bigger by 1 ogg, the remainder of the octave − a perfect fourth − also has to be reduced by 1 ogg or it wouldn't fit in to an octave! Similarly with a minor third (+ 8 oggs) and a major third (− 7 oggs) to fit into a perfect fifth. The intervals have to be adjusted.

To sum up: read this section again if you are not sure of it. Playing in tune means being able to adjust in the right direction according to the pitch of the other players *or* the surrounding notes. You are not taking a step back into the past. Equal Temperament is here to stay. Clear recognition of Just Temperament enables you to *play* in Equal Temperament *or*, to make slight adjustments according to the circumstances in order to play *better* than Equal Temperament. Put another way, to play *really* in tune.

Finally, the adjustment to the intonation refers to the key you are in. When the piece changes key, the adjustments change, though you will probably not get as far as that stage. It will be found sufficient to *appreciate* the necessary adjustments in the present key.

The following piece is a good example of changing intonation. The changes are *only small.* The asterisks indicate the notes you should be most conscious of. As the piano part is largely arpeggios it is not so important to play each flute note at the same pitch as the piano. If, however, the piano part has block chords – as illustrated for simplicity in the example below – then playing each note at the same pitch as the piano *would* be necessary. You will have to use your judgement as to when it sounds more beautiful to play out of tune with the piano!

MADRIGAL

P. GAUBERT

DIFFERENCE TONES

Now the proof, using your flute. For this next experiment you will need another flute player. The two flutes should be played *without vibrato* or any kind of wobble. Tune the two flutes perfectly to the upper D played forte. Whilst player one is holding his D, player two should play B♭ below it. Immediately an uncomfortable buzz will be heard, the result of interaction between the two notes. This buzz will, on careful listening, be apparent as a very flat B♭ sounding nearly two octaves below. It is a Difference Tone. It is called a Difference Tone because it is a note which sounds as a result of hearing two simultaneous clear tones; it is the mathematical *difference* between the two notes.

At concert pitch (A=440 Hz.), the pitch of the two notes is:
D=1174.6 Hz. (cycles per second)
B♭=932.3 Hz.

Subtract one from the other, the difference being 242.3 Hz. which is a little flatter than a B♮ two octaves below. (B♮ is 246.9 Hz.). If you *like* a chord of B♮ + B♭ + D – O.K.! Most people don't, so *reduce* the size of the major third either by sharpening the B♭ or flattening D until the difference tone becomes B♭ exactly two octaves below the B♭ played by the second flute. The chord will then sound in tune.

Notice that raising the lower note or flattening the higher note of any interval *flattens* the Difference Tone.
Now for another three-part chord played by two flutes:
1st flute plays high D again and
2nd flute plays B♮ below it.

The result is a minor third. But another note way below can be heard. Subtract B from D.

D = 1174.6 Hz.
B = 987.8 Hz.

186.8 Hz.

This gives a difference tone of 186.8 which is very close to F♯ in the low register. What we need to do to make the two notes sound sweet and in tune is to make the F♯ Difference Tone rise to a G♮. To make the difference tone *rise*, the interval has to be made larger. Therefore, the 2nd flute, who plays the B♮, must flatten it with his lips until the Difference Tone – F♯ – rises to G♮, giving a perfect triad of G Major.

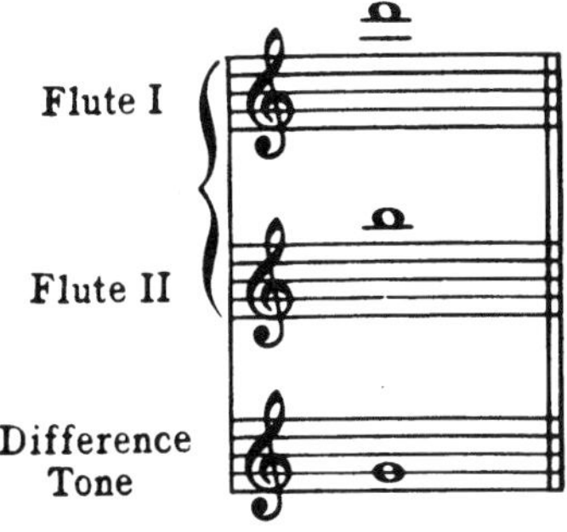

To reinforce this point, all intervals produce Difference Tones which can only clearly be heard when the instruments playing them have few, if any, natural harmonics in the tone. Two oboes would be useless for this experiment as they have many natural harmonics sounding with the fundamental.

To further illustrate Difference Tones, here are three trios for two flutes! Careful examination of the chart on page 11 and a careful adjustment of the requisite Oggs will produce the bass line illustrated in the first two trios. Memorise the Oggs chart and use your ears. It is better for one player only to make these adjustments.

ARBEAU-WARLOCK

GOD SAVE THE QUEEN

In this 'trio' the tune appears in the Difference Tones. What is the tune?

Try writing your own trio for two flutes!

Have you been wondering why equal temperament tuning hasn't worried you, or others before you? It has, though music has become so harmonically complex that the differences don't show as much as in earlier, purer music.

Fifty years ago a lecturer on music said 'The human ear is much like the back of a donkey; you can whip it into callousness to almost any kind of harmonic punishment.' How very true that is today.

THE FLUTE SCALE

Before we go further, a close examination should be made of the scale of your flute. During the past fifteen years, manufacturers have gone through a period of re-examination in many aspects of flute making, notably the tone-hole positions or flute scale.

When Boehm designed the modern flute in 1847 he developed a precise method of calculating the position of the tone holes and hence, the intonation.

The pitch in use at this time was A=435 Hz. or cycles per second. Gradually, between 1847 and 1930 the pitch generally in use rose to A=440 Hz. Though the flute makers made adjustments to the scale, such as moving the A♮ hole closer to the mouth hole, a rise in pitch would require *all* the tone holes to be moved. Each manufacturer found his own method of doing this and not until fairly recently did any re-examination of the complete scale take place, largely due to the work of Albert Cooper of London. He devised a scale which lowered the traditionally sharp notes in the left hand (C♯ and C♮ etc.) and raised the flat notes at the lower end of the flute. The result is Cooper's Scale, a new scheme for the size and position of the tone holes to enable us to play an Equal Tempered scale without having to make big adjustments with the lips. It is enough to have to do battle with draughty halls, differently pitched pianos, the temperature of the room, and the problems of other players, without having the added problem of one's own flute.

A modern scale flute such as Cooper's will not solve *all* problems. Adjustments will still have to be made in different performing conditions. In general, a traditional scale flute is sharp on some left hand notes and flat in the right hand lower notes, or expressed another way, the octave length of the flute is too long. At the time of this revision, 1991, most manufacturers have adopted the new scale flutes, some completely, and some with their own modifications.

Check it yourself. First, tune carefully to a tuning fork, then play low C followed by the first harmonic of C. Then slur to the natural left hand fingering of C:

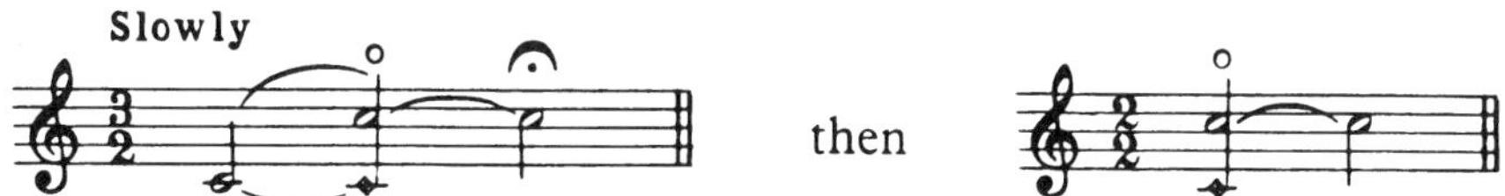

There is a change of tone quality but the notes should be in tune. MAKE NO ATTEMPT TO TUNE THE NOTES WITH YOUR LIPS.

Repeat with C♯:

Do the upper C's and C♯'s appear to be sharper than the harmonics? They shouldn't be. If they are, the chances are that your flute is a traditional scale flute. But first, some further checks. If you've already read the section headed THE CHORD OF NATURE you will realise that a perfect fifth is a *near* perfect interval in Equal Temperament. Therefore, also check the fifths:

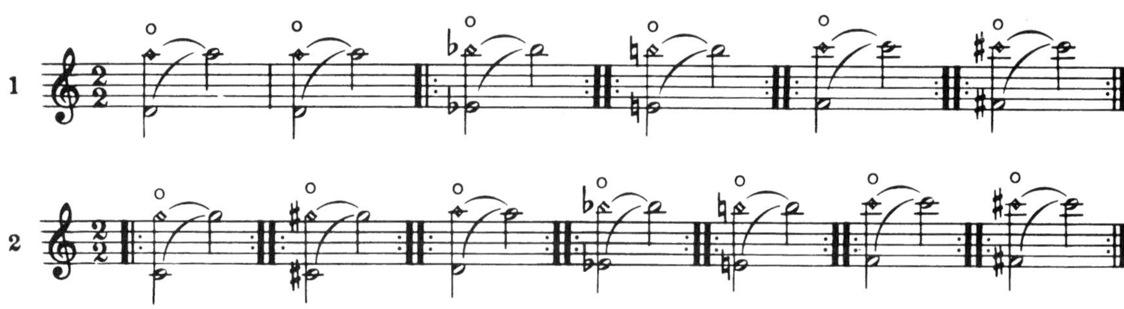

Be sure *not* to move your lips in an attempt to tune the notes. The normal fingering should sound very slightly flat. (1 Ogg!)

Some flutes have, in the left hand fingering a *sharp* C♯ and a *flat* C♮. These popular flutes also have a short headjoint which complicates things. A temporary remedy is to pull the headjoint out somewhat, though that will make the C♮ flatter still! After careful checking, if your flute seems to need some adjustment you could, if it is a good flute, have the tone holes moved and tuned – a costly business.

Although the right hand notes can't be made sharper, the left hand notes, C♯, and C♮, and B♭ *can* be made flatter. With flatter left hand notes, the headjoint can be pushed further in thus raising the pitch of the right hand notes.

Even with a modern scale flute, you may wish to adjust it slightly. Don't stop using your ears, even with a modern scale flute!

POSITIONS OF TONE HOLES CHART

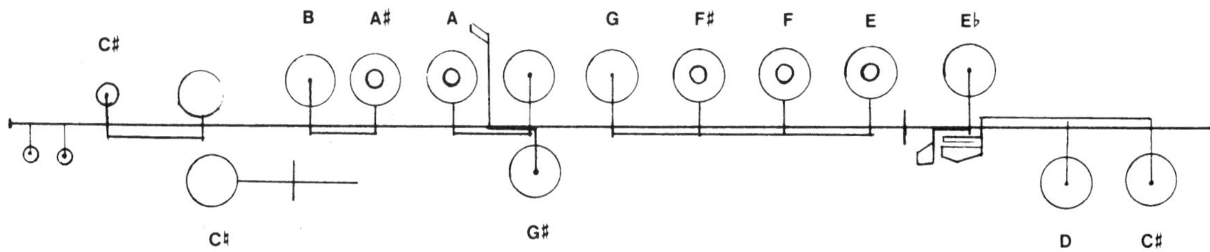

Make a list of notes which you feel are a little sharp. Study the diagram above.
To make some adjustments to your flute you will need some plasticine and a toothpick or sharpened matchstick. Remove left hand mechanism and thumb key (C♮ tone hole). Roll a piece of plasticine between your fingers and thumb and wipe it against the inside edge of the required tone hole as labelled in the diagram, leaving a crescent shaped deposit as shown:

HEAD JOINT ←—— ◐ ——→ FOOT JOINT

By doing this the vibrating column of air will have further to travel down the tube before escaping and so the note will be flatter. Sculpt the plasticine carefully with a toothpick and remove any from the top of the tone hole so that on replacing the key, the pad will not come into contact with the plasticine. Replace the mechanism. Try the tuning exercise again. If further adjustments are necessary, add or subtract more plasticine.

These adjustments to the tuning will not affect the tone to any discernible degree.
Don't worry about lumps appearing in the bore of the flute. Do not swab out your flute. When satisfied, play it for a week. Then, replace the plasticine (some of which may have fallen out anyway) with a fibre-glass paste or a car body repair paste, widely available. This substance can be scraped or filed away to fine-tune the note. It can also, if required, easily be removed by exerting pressure on it when dried. This technique has a two-fold effect on the scale: it causes the air column to travel farther and it makes the hole smaller, both of which flatten a note.

Some further checks:

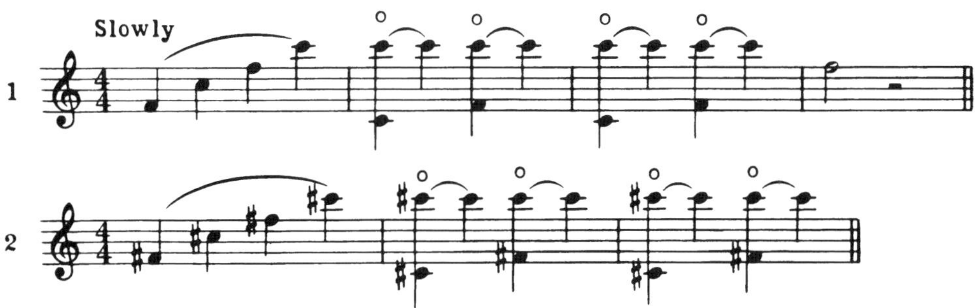

It is quite impossible to say what should be done to *your* flute. Each maker has a different scale. Generally speaking, however, traditional scale flutes have a very sharp C♯ and C♮ and a quite sharp A♯ in the left hand. Only F♯ is often sharp in the right hand. From F♮ down, the notes get progressively flatter.

N.B. Be sure the cork in the headjoint is correctly placed. It should be 17.3 mm from the centre of the embouchure hole. Most cleaning sticks have a line engraved at this point which should appear in the *centre* of the embouchure hole. It should *never* be moved from this position as it affects the TONE throughout the entire compass and the intonation of the third octave from D upwards.
The point of this section is, then, to flatten any sharp notes. Flat notes can't be sharpened, but flattening the sharp notes and pushing the head joint further in, will sharpen *all* the notes. If necessary, half of a centimetre could be cut off the socket end of the headjoint to enable the head to be pushed in more, though do take note of the last two paragraphs of the section headed TUNING UP.

PERFECT PITCH

Many players claim to have perfect pitch.

Perfect or absolute pitch is the ability to identify a musical sound accurately without the help of a reference sound. *This ability is rare.* The ability to identify a note by comparison with a remembered note is common and can be acquired with a little effort. This is called relative pitch. Carry a tuning fork around and practise comparing everyday sounds with it. For a few months listen to the tuning fork before going to sleep. After some practice, you will easily recall the pitch of the fork at any time.

TUNING UP

Musical performances are often spoiled by the inability of the young student to tune correctly. Look at these portraits to see if you can recognise yourself:

1 The player and pianist walk on to the platform. The pianist plays an A which is a signal for the flute player to blot out the note he has heard by performing a few short rapid scales or loud random notes. No adjustment to the flute is made. He coughs. He adjusts his music and his tie. After sucking his teeth, he starts to play.

2 This is the timid one; he plays a staccatissimo, pianissimo A, peers down the flute like a telescope, as if he is Vasco da Gama sighting land; nods confidently to the pianist and begins.

3 As above, only this is a more experienced player; he has observed what professional players do at recitals and he imitates their method of warming up. Offstage can be heard the final variation of the 'Carnival of Tunis'; the audience waits expectantly. He walks on; the pianist plays an A, which the flautist disdains; it must be the wrong flavour! He minutely examines a part of the mechanism and nods to the pianist. Very impressive until he begins the first phrase.

The whole object of tuning up is to *tune up*. No player, however advanced, can hope to give a good performance and give pleasure to his audience without first establishing a pitch relationship with the other player or players.

Most often the performer cannot hear the pitch easily and, feeling that he *ought* to be able to, tries to cover his inadequacy. Allow me, please, to let you into a secret: TUNING UP WITH ANY INSTRUMENT, *particularly* THE PIANO, IS NOT EASY. You are not the only one!

Now to practicalities.

How is the tuning best done? Assuming that the section in the front of this book has been carefully read, tuning up becomes easier with a little practice. You must start from the mental position of *not knowing whether you are sharp, flat, or in tune*. Don't try to understand too quickly or you will not understand at all. The problem is to compare, assess and adjust with the pitch of another instrument.

'If I don't know I don't know
I think I know.
If I don't know I know
I think I don't know.'

KNOTS – R. D. LAING
(reprinted by permission Tavistock Publications Ltd)

Try it this way using the upper A:

Make a judgement: are you sharper, flatter, or the same as the two outside notes? If in doubt, guess. Then adjust and repeat. Again, make a judgement. Don't wait. Make an *immediate* judgement, right or wrong. Then, adjust accordingly and repeat. Do this until you are satisfied. *Make certain you are playing with the same sound as when playing your solo*. If, during the piece, you feel that the pitch is still not correct, then re-adjust during some bars' rest or at the end of the movement. A slow, quiet movement may sound slightly flatter than you would wish; before playing slow movements, push the head *in* a little, though do remember to pull the head out again for the last movement. Don't be ashamed or embarrassed about tuning up in public. Take your time.

For the flute, A♮ is not a very satisfactory note to tune to. You will get a better idea of the total tuning by repeating the above with middle D instead of A.
Be in no doubt as to what happens when the head joint is pushed in:
Suppose you tune to C♮ in the left hand, and, sounding flat, you push the head in by 1 cm to sharpen it. The distance from the mouth hole to the C♮ hole is about 27 cm. You have, therefore, shortened the distance to C by 1/27th. The lower C – an octave lower – which has a tube length of about 60 cm has been shortened by 1/60th. As 1/27th is the *greater fraction*, the upper C will have been sharpened by roughly *twice* the amount of the lower C.
When tuning, therefore, it is wise to tune both A and D, lest when pulling out for A, the D becomes too flat.
This underlines the point that a flute can ideally only be constructed to be played at one pitch. One could go further and say that it can only be played at one pitch, by one player at one temperature. Anything else is a compromise. Therefore, D would be a more practical note to tune to after checking A.

VIBRATO

Vibrato is a fluctuation in the flute tone, about three quarters of which is a rise and fall in pitch, the remainder, a rise and fall in volume or loudness.
Read through this section first to see what it entails.
It has been said that vibrato is something a performer should *feel*, not something to be learned. For those who feel it – and produce vibrato naturally – this may be true. For the large majority who can't do it and want to know *how* to do it, it is something that should be studied and correctly learnt. *String players study vibrato in great detail.*
Vibrato has only been in universal use during this century. In the eighteenth century it was used on some long notes as an ornament. During the early part of the nineteenth century, its use increased to marking the high points in a phrase. With the wide acceptance of the Boehm flute, its use increased though each country developed its own vibrato style. In the advent of Impressionism, it was more widely used and has now become part of the normal colouring of flute tone.
If you were to study the vibrato of singers and players you would notice that vibrato rarely goes above seven wobbles and rarely below four wobbles per second. *It is desirable to vary the vibrato according to the mood and the speed of the music, and the octave in which one is playing.*
The exercises which follow will train you in the use of vibrato between 4 and 7 wobbles per second.
There are three basic ways of producing a fluctuation in pitch:
(a) by moving the lips or jaw by alternately compressing and relaxing the lips.
(b) by opening and shutting the throat.
(c) by using the larynx.
(d) by fluctuating the air speed and therefore the air pressure with the diaphragm.

(c) and (d) are jointly the method most commonly used and are recommended because:
(i) it allows the lips solely to perform the function of forming the embouchure.
(ii) it allows the throat to remain open and relaxed – probably the most important single factor in tone production.
(iii) it encourages the correct use of the diaphragm for tonal support.
Vibrato is a regular equal rise and fall in the pitch of a note. Rise *and* fall. If the vibrato only rises *above* the note, the ear hears the average or mean pitch which would be sharper.
Remember that the flute was once played without vibrato. The production of a clear straight tone is essential before adding any wobble.

STAGE ONE

Play a few long notes without any fluctuation in pitch. Use the abdominal muscles as in sighing. If any involuntary, unwanted vibrato is already being produced, try to eliminate it or see the Problem Box at the end of this section.

When your tone is straight, play a low G holding the flute only with the left hand. Place your right hand on your abdomen and push and relax your right hand alternately rhythmically to achieve an increase and decrease in air speed. Start at about two or three wobbles per second. It is similar to silently saying ha, ha, ha, ha. (See the diagram below.)

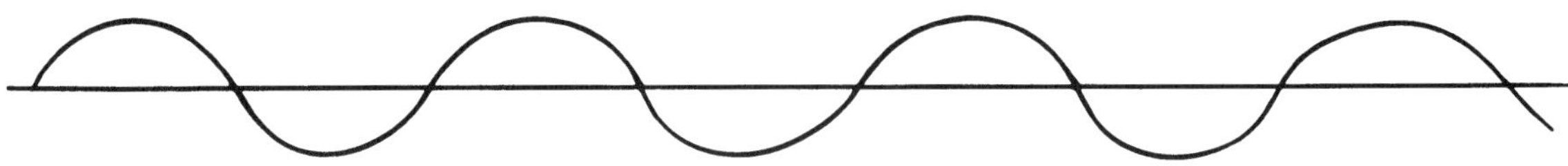

When this is working, try to achieve the same result with the abdominal muscles only, holding the flute with both hands. *The movement of the air must be continuous, not a series of jerks.*

The movement in pitch, too, must go above and below the straight note. *Do* not at this stage assist the vibrato in any way with the throat, lips, arms, or shoulders. Keep still. Persevere with this exercise until it can be done with ease. This may take a few days or a few minutes; do not proceed until you can do this easily. Now play the scale of G, pulsing eight times on each note. Choose a tempo which suits you then try after a time to increase to ♩ =90. Don't let the width of the vibrato get narrower in the middle and upper registers.

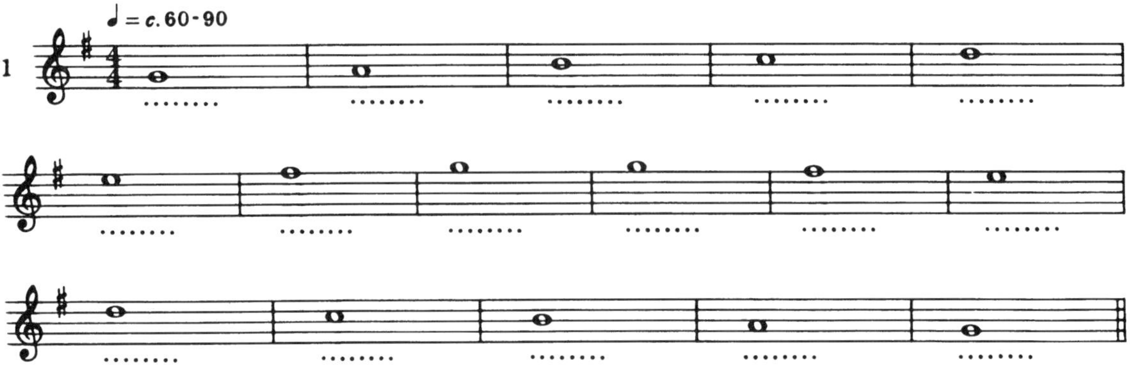

Often the vibrato stops as the note changes. Try to overcome this. Now repeat with six pulses on each note.

Two or three separate ten-minute sessions on these exercises per day will soon produce results. Don't go on until the previous exercise becomes easy.

Time, patience and intelligent work.

Now gradually increase the speed, adding slurs: three wobbles per crotchet.

Be patient: some may find it more difficult than others. Next, find some tunes (hymn-tunes are ideal) in which there are no dotted notes, relatively fast-moving notes, or large leaps i.e.:

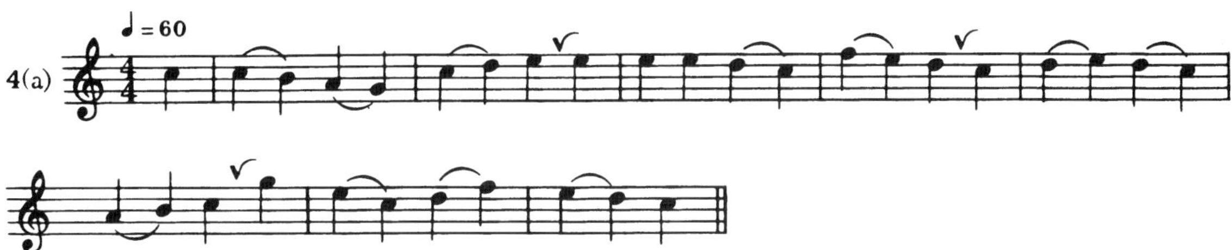

Count four pulses (or even six if played very slowly) on each note.
Practise many times each day.
Now for a tune with small leaps. Keep the vibrato moving during the quavers:

Don't stop the vibrato between notes.
Here is another:

PRAISE TO THE HOLIEST IN THE HEIGHT

Adapted from T. HAWEIS, 1734–1820, by S. WEBBE

It is a little more difficult to produce the vibrato in the upper register; practise this one carefully. Keep the vibrato going during the quavers:

LET US, WITH A GLADSOME MIND

Melody from Hymn-tunes of the United Brethren, 1824

The minimum time to have spent on the above and previous exercises would be about three weeks; some of you will find a longer time is necessary.

STAGE TWO

Vibrato should not be mechanical and calculated. To progress from Stage One to Stage Two involves trying to allow the vibrato to be a *part of the tone* and not something added to it.

It is a common problem at this point to choose the speed of the notes to suit the speed of the vibrato. In other words you will find your fingers moving after every fourth or sixth wobble even if the piece is slightly unrhythmic as a result.

How to overcome this:

1) Play one of the tunes in this way: play the first note *without counting the pulses of vibrato* and slur on to the next note unpredictably. Some will find this easy, others not. Then play through the tune using much vibrato but changing notes without reference to the pulses of vibrato.

2) Play through your tunes using five pulses to each crotchet, and during the piece, if you happen to use four or six, well, it doesn't matter, does it?

The whole idea of these two ways is to allow the vibrato to be free of the rhythm of the notes so that – like forte and piano – it can become another cosmetic in your musical make-up bag, to be used in the service of music making.

At this stage you may have observed that the abdominal muscles are causing the larynx or throat to pulse in sympathy. This is fine, but *don't assist this throat movement by any sort of tension.* Just let it happen. Little by little the larynx will take over a large part of the work. Any forcing of the throat at this point will result in what was called in the eighteenth century CHEVROTEMENT or a bleating goat vibrato. Save *that* for your old age!

STAGE THREE

(a) Play this exercise. Use vibrato *through* the quavers. Keep the vibrato moving all the time:

(b) Choose other tunes with dotted notes, quavers, etc. but not fast tunes. Be sure the vibrato is ever present particularly on the long notes. For example:

GOD THAT MADEST EARTH AND HEAVEN

Traditional Welsh

You are over the worst; hereafter it's just practice. You, the player, may feel that the vibrato sounds mechanical but your listeners will soon dispel these doubts. This mechanical feeling will soon vanish and vibrato will become part of your tone.

STAGE FOUR

Try to bend *low* C downwards to lower its pitch as much as possible. (See Practice Book Vol 1, page 34). You will be lucky to achieve a true B♮. Now do the same to C an octave higher (left hand C). You may well be able to bend this note down to B♭ or A♮. The blowing tube becomes shorter as you ascend the scale of C and the notes become more sensitive to pitch change. This is important in vibrato practice.

Play the scale of G again:

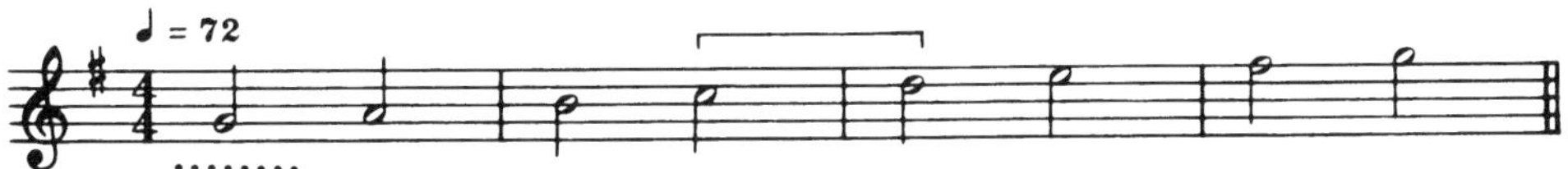

Without your doing anything to assist it, from G to C the vibrato becomes increasingly wider and, on changing to D, narrower again. It is more difficult to use a wide vibrato when the tube is long.
Therefore, practise slow scales to try to maintain the same *pitch change in the vibrato* throughout the scale.

Try other scales as well.
Practise slow scales now throughout the entire compass. The top register may prove to be more difficult and special attention to this register is necessary.

STAGE FIVE

Practise the vibrato at up to and including seven wobbles *per second.* It may begin to even out at six per second until there is an almost straight note. Practice of the earlier exercises, with a wider pitch change will first be necessary. Gradually increase the speed of the wobbles per second.
A metronome is quite indispensable for this.

STAGE SIX

Vibrato should be present but perhaps to a less noticeable degree in moderately moving quavers (say four per second) otherwise the vibrato sticks out as only being used on long notes. Therefore practise this next exercise first very slowly, with a noticeable vibrato, and increase the speed of the rhythm *without stopping the vibrato* until ♩ =*c.*132.

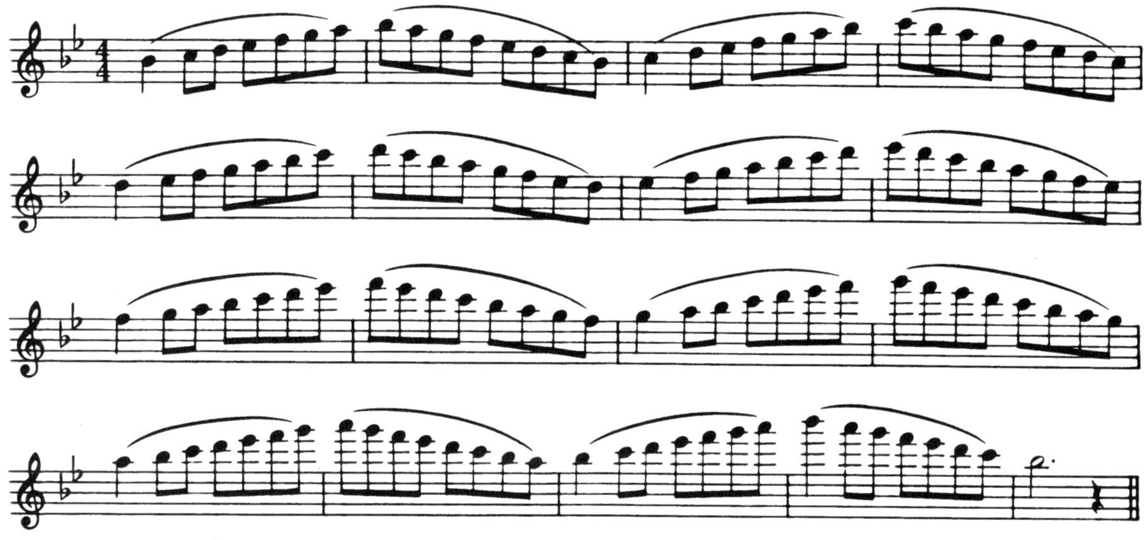

At this point it can *almost* be said that the wobble has disappeared and in its place is a new-found means of expression.
The rest is up to you.

PROBLEMS BOX

1) Vibrato should be *within* and inside the tone, not added on top. If your tone is small, the vibrato should remain within it. Don't transplant the heart of an elephant into a mouse!

2) If your vibrato was achieved naturally and without thinking about it – lucky you. You shouldn't be reading this box because you have no problems! You may however like to join in at any of the stages to *improve* your vibrato.

3) If your vibrato sounds like a goat:

B-aaaaaaaa!

spend a week or two playing long straight notes, at the end of which start Stage One. In all probability, your throat is tense.

4) Watch yourself in a mirror whilst practising. Are your lips moving? Shoulders? Arms? They shouldn't be.

5) A note should start with vibrato. Many pop and folk singers start a note straight, then add vibrato: this makes the performance gimmicky. Avoid it.

FINALLY
When should vibrato be learned? When the tone has been reasonably developed, though it should not be learned simply to paint over obvious flaws. Most young players seem to adjust easily to learning vibrato after two or three years learning the flute, some even sooner.

Experiment with your new-found expression. Slow, low register tunes may sound best with a gently languid vibrato: exciting tunes, especially in the middle and high register may sound better with a faster vibrato.

Occasionally play some eighteenth-century sonata without vibrato. You may well be called upon to do that in an orchestra some day. It is important to be able to play with little or none on occasions. 'The Dance of the Blessed Spirits' (*Orfeo* – Gluck), a pure, ethereal, gentle melody, can sound beautiful in this way. It too often sounds like the hip-swinging dance of a scantily clad chorus girl.

Flute playing is always on the move; changes in style and tone are more obvious examples of changing taste. In the next fifty years one of the changes that must surely come is the control and damping down of vibrato. Its over-use today, especially in eighteenth- and nineteenth-century music, is most apparent in many orchestras where the flutes can often be heard bleating above the throng.

TWENTY FOUR STUDIES FOR INTONATION

Of course, any exercise, played slowly, can become a study for intonation.
These short exercises, one in each key, have used the most common intervals to help you develop a keen 'ear'. They are in order of key but not in order of difficulty; you will decide for yourself which are the most difficult.
Pay particular attention – even with a 'tuned' flute – to the left hand C♯'s and C♮'s, and to the lowest notes.
Most of the exercises should be repeated on octave higher where a different set of problems will arise. *Avoid playing sharp in the top register.*
Practise these studies both piano and forte, and always slowly.

A minor

Practise one octave higher

G major

Practise one octave higher

E minor

Practise one octave higher

D major

Practise one octave higher

B minor

Practise one octave higher

A major

F♯ minor

E major

C♯ minor

B major

G♯ minor

12

Practise one octave higher

F♯ major

13

Practise one octave higher

E♭ minor

14

B♭ minor

Practise one octave higher

D♭ major

Practise one octave higher

F minor

Practise one octave higher

A♭ major

Practise one octave higher

C minor

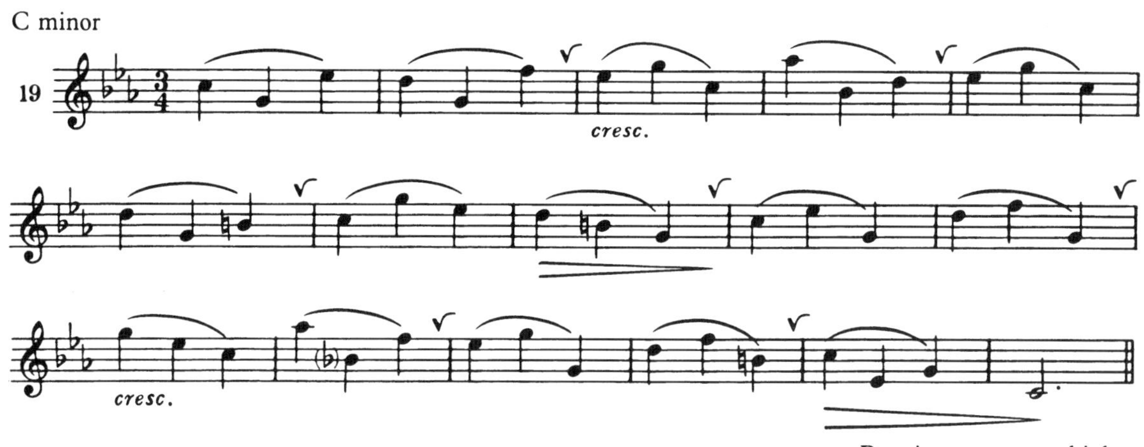

Practise one octave higher

E♭ major

Practise one octave higher

G minor

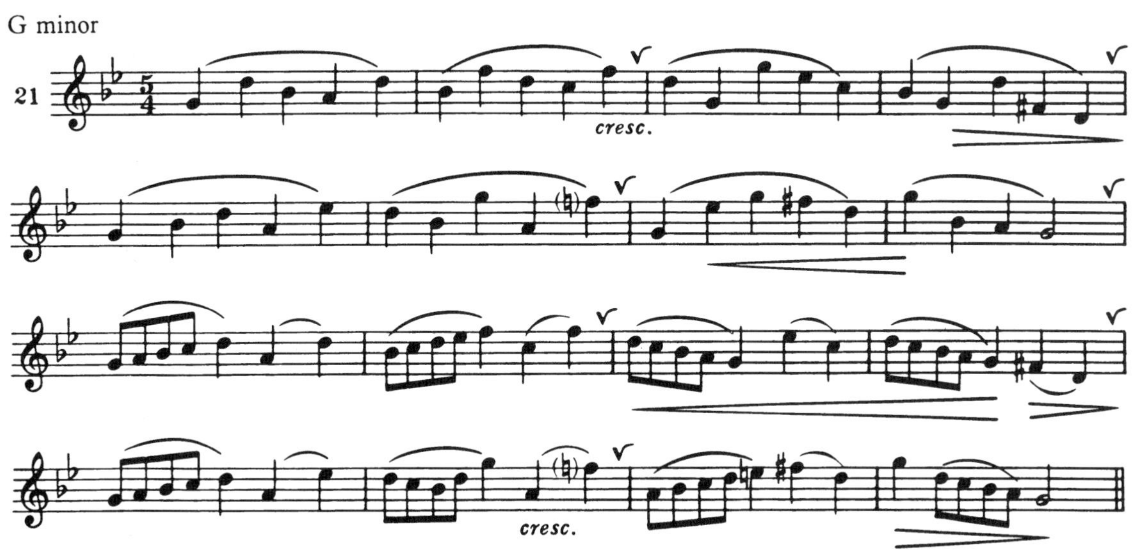

Practise one octave higher

B♭ major

Practise one octave higher

F major

Practise one octave higher

D minor

Practise one octave higher

A useful study for intonation is the Tone Colour Exercise in Volume 1 – TONE in this series. It should be practised in all keys.

EXAMPLES OF INTONATION PROBLEMS IN MUSICAL WORKS

For the advanced player, the fingering chart as found in beginner's books is no longer relevant.

There are many special fingerings which resolve some of the problems of intonation. *The 'correct' fingering is the one that is most in tune.*

Here are some examples of possible – or should I say probable! – intonation problems in the orchestral repertoire. Study of these scores in the light of what has been learned will ease many of the difficulties.

I am indebted to Messrs. Roger Rostron and Colin Chambers for assistance in compiling this list.

Top of the list: Mendelssohn *Midsummer Night's Dream Overture.*

2) Rimsky-Korsakov
   (a) *Sheherazade* – see also bars 314-320, 362-376, 394-401. 1st movement, bar 8 (similar to above). Bars 228 to end in E Major.
   (b) Triplet figure at bar 102 (D).
   (c) 4th movement, bar 655 to the end. The harmonics from 1st desk of violins add problems.

3) Ravel
   Bolero – two piccolo variations.

4) Shostakovich
   (a) *Symphony No. 5* – 1st movement, bar after (39) solo with horn.
   (b) *Symphony No. 10* – 1st movement, two piccolos at end of movement.
   (c) 3rd movement, flute and piccolo in octaves.

5) Tchaikovsky
   (a) *Nutcracker Suite* – 'Dance de Mirlitons' – bar 4: arpeggio.
   (b) *Symphony No. 5* – 4th movement, beginning with bassoons.

6) Verdi
   (a) *Force of Destiny Overture* – bars 51-66, tuning with Oboe and Clarinet.
   (b) *Sicilian Vespers Overture* – bars 14-33, tuning with two clarinets and bass clarinet in E Major.
   (c) *Requiem* – end of 'Lux Aeterna' *pp* to top B♭.

7) Beethoven
   (a) *Leonora No. 3 Overture* – bars 1-5, 278-294, 301-315, 352-360.
   (b) *Symphony No. 7* – 1st movement, bars 56-67 and until 136.
   (c) *Piano Concerto No. 5 (Emperor)* – slow movement.

8) Brahms
   (a) *Symphony No. 1* – 1st movement, bars 1-15.
   (b) 3rd movement, bars 150 to end, but especially bar 162.
   (c) Many of Brahms' Symphonies have movements which end in restrained chords which need careful adjustment.

9) Debussy
   La Mer – 3rd movement, six bars after 54: long solo with oboe.

10) Dvorak
   (a) *Symphony No. 9 (New World)* – 2nd movement figure (1) for six bars.
   (b) 4th movement after the solo, a long diminuendo.

11) Mendelssohn
   Hebrides Overture – last three bars.

12) Mozart
   Piano Concertos – the late ones have prominent wind parts. When the piano has not been tuned to A=440, it can play havoc with the woodwind particularly the clarinets and bassoons which in turn create more problems for the poor flute player.

13) Wagner
   Tannhäuser Overture – bars 82-94 and 184-190: tendency to get sharp with crescendo.

VIRTUS IN ARDUIS: Valour in difficulties!

TREVOR WYE

OMNIBUS EDITION BOOKS 1-5

PRACTICE BOOKS for the *flute*

VOLUME 5

Breathing and Scales

CONTENTS

BREATHING
BREATHING AND YOUR BODY

Firstly, assuming that you have survived to read this sentence, there really can't be much wrong with the way you breathe, though to play a few notes on a pipe as the ancients did is simple; the requirements of modern flute playing, of composers, and therefore of the musical phrase, demand that more detailed attention be paid to the way we breathe.

What is curious is that we breathe most naturally when horizontal; this is our most relaxed position. Any breathing difficulties are experienced when standing upright.

Wind players need lots of air in their lungs and they need the utmost control over its intake and expulsion. The flute player uses more air than any other wood-wind player; for that reason alone it is necessary to ensure that this basic process is correctly learned.

It is not proposed here to go into the medical mechanics of taking and expelling breath, which could be misleading, confusing, unhelpful and even downright daft. You don't need to know all the precise mechanical processes taking place in a car in order to drive one. A fully explanatory article (of which there are many) with copious, revolting, medical diagrams should be read by the dead who have a desperate need to know of such matters, or by the insatiably curious living. Here we will confine ourselves to an examination only of what is strictly necessary for flute playing.

Of the many opinions about breathing, one clear point emerges, namely that it is wrong to raise the shoulders when taking in a breath. The reasons will become clearer when you start the exercises. It is wrong because (a) it tightens the throat and often leads to (b) a bleating, goat-like vibrato (see Practice Book 4, Page 22) which, in turn usually (c) encourages the development of grunts, or vocal cord noises, whilst playing. Raising the shoulders also (d) makes it impossible to properly control the expulsion of air from the lungs and (e) it conflicts with the way in which the flute tone should develop with regard to the mouth and throat cavities (see TONE in Practice Book 6).

In short, don't.

The rib cage contains the lungs. The rib bones are fastened to the spine at the back, and to the breast bone in front. The breast bone divides into two branches half way down your front. Because of this division, the lower ribs are able to expand to some extent; the upper ones less so, though due to the softness and flexibility of bones and tissues, they have some outward movement. Underneath both lungs is a membrane, not unlike a muscular drum skin, called the *diaphragm*. The muscles of the diaphragm can be tightened or relaxed. When tightened, the diaphragm flattens; when it relaxes, it resumes its natural position which is dome-shaped in an upward direction. Muscles can only work in one direction – by contracting. When contracted, the dome-shaped diaphragm flattens and thus draws air into the lungs. The *abdominal muscles* are used to expel the air from the lungs. With your hand on your abdomen you can feel these muscles by tightening them and relaxing them as in coughing, or laughing.
A normal breath involves tightening the diaphragm to pull the lungs downwards; this creates a vacuum in the lungs causing air to rush in through the mouth. *Relaxing* the diaphragm and *tightening* the abdominal muscles will push the diaphragm back into its upwards dome-shape, thus expelling the air.

That is about as much air as is necessary for a big sigh; for flute playing more is needed, which is why some exercises must be done.

EXERCISE I

Place your hand on your abdomen; when breathing in, your abdomen should move out; when breathing out, it should move back in.* You should become thinner when breathing out, and fatter when breathing in.

Now place your hands on your hips but reverse your hand position so that the outside, or back, of the wrists is against your pelvic bone with the palms of the hands facing outwards. Now take a breath as before pushing the abdomen outwards but this time continuing to take in air by *expanding the rib cage sideways.*

You become *wider*, not *taller*. These diagrams may help you understand.

Let's assume the lungs are like a box:—

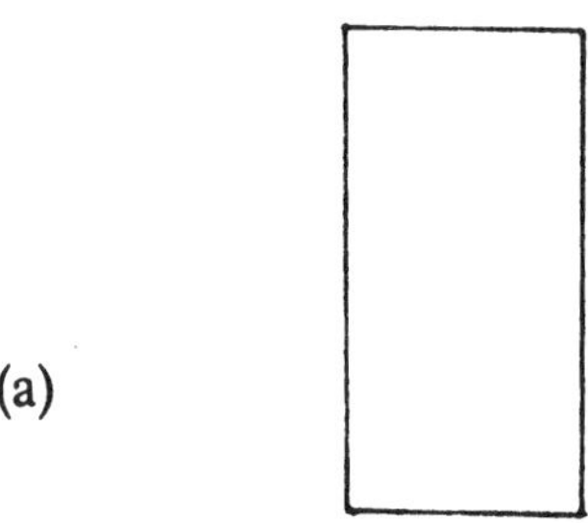

(a)

When a gentle breath is taken in, the lower part expands:—

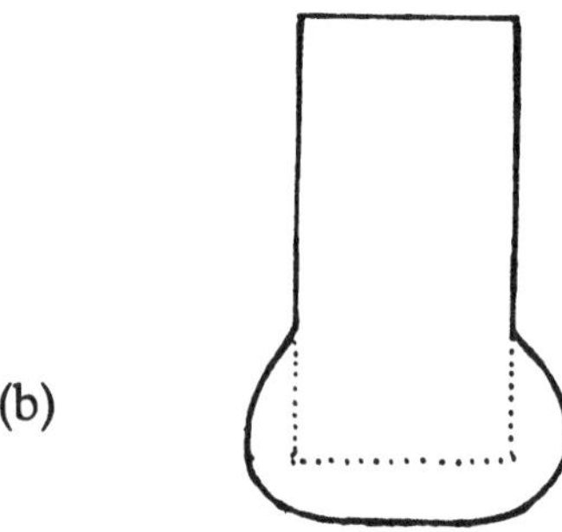

(b)

When a large breath is taken in, with the rib-cage expanding sideways, it would look like:—

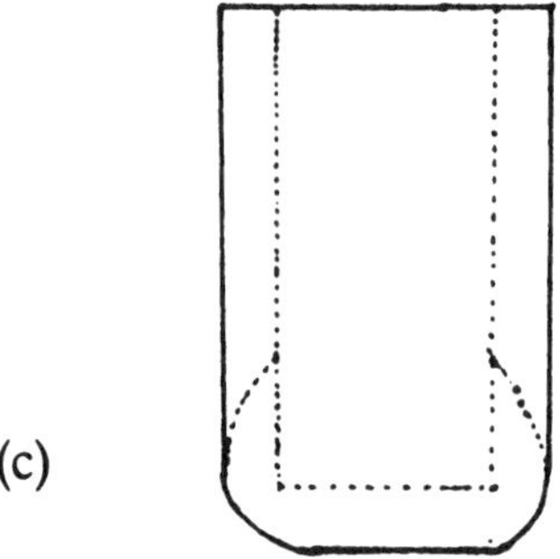

(c)

*If you have any difficulty experiencing this, sit in an upright chair, fold your body forward until your hands touch the ground and your abdomen is resting on your thighs. Breathe in and raise yourself slightly as you do so. You should feel the pressure of your abdomen on your thighs. *Or* lie flat on the floor. Place a book on your abdomen, gently breathe in and out raising the book when breathing *in*.

If the shoulders were raised, it would look like:—

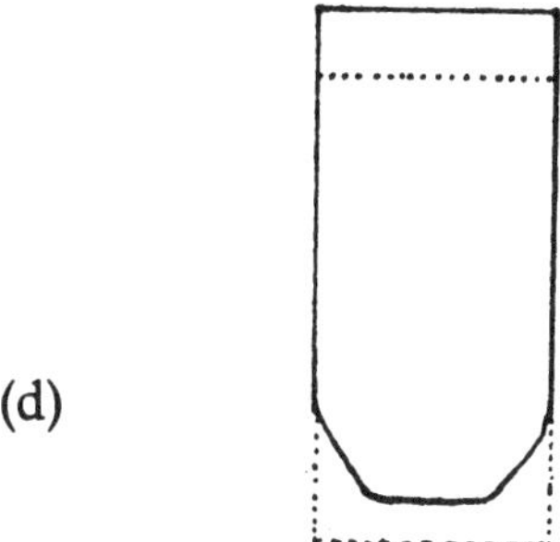

Observe how the abdomen becomes thinner when the shoulders are raised.

So far, this should be quite straightforward. Unfortunately, the position in which the flute is held tends to encourage shoulder-breathing, especially for beginners who, in their first few weeks, attempt to support the head-joint with the left shoulder.*

Look in a mirror. Is your rib cage going upwards when breathing in? It shouldn't be. Are you raising your shoulders?

Just to check: with your hands hanging by your sides, (a) take a deep breath deliberately raising the shoulders and holding your abdomen in, (b) place your wrists on your hips and repeat the breath, expanding first your abdomen and secondly, your rib cage. See the difference?

Take up your flute and play long notes checking at each breath that the shoulders are down when breathing in, and the throat is relaxed. Use a mirror.

Play some pieces and check yourself often. For the proper control of the air supply, Exercise I is sufficient for the time being.

For 'support' of the flute tone and to obtain that singing quality, especially in the third octave, you will need to refer to the Tone Section in Practice Book 6 dealing with abdominal tension, where it is fully explained.

For a *really* large intake of air you will need to practise Exercise II which is set out in the next section, LONGEVITY.

*Correct posture is essential to correct breathing, especially the flute/body relationship, and the left hand and arm position (see Beginners' Book for Flute – Novello; also in Practice Book 6).

BREATHING AND LUNGEVITY

Your lungs are capable of expanding far in excess of the size of your chest; the problem is that the ribs prevent them. This section concerns increasing the expansion and contraction of the ribs so that the lungs can accommodate more air. *It's the difference between the expansion and contraction of your ribs which directly affects how long you can play without taking another breath.*

EXERCISE II

Place your hands backwards on your hips. Start by breathing out all the air in your lungs. *All* the air, not just most of it. Yes, really; *all* of it! It *should* feel uncomfortable. Now breathe in slowly through your nose. Start filling the abdomen first then expand the ribs outwards. You may also feel your back filling out. Take in the *maximum* that you can. *Do not breathe out:* now take a bit more. *Yes you can!* and a bit more, *and a bit more still.* Hold it. Now breathe out slowly. Get rid of every bit of air in your lungs, keep breathing out until it feels painful. Now relax. Begin again. Repeat six times.

The whole exercise cycle feels a little uncomfortable, doesn't it? Your ribs aren't used to such big movements. Ask a friend with a tape measure to measure your capacity. The tape goes around your chest a couple of inches or so below your arm-pits. Expel *all* the air. Take a reading. Take in as much air as possible expanding your ribs. Take another reading. The *difference* between the two readings is your expansion.

Untrained, your expansion is likely to be between one and two inches (2.5 – 5 cms). Write it down on this table:

MONTH	YEAR	EXPANSION
JANUARY		
FEBRUARY		
MARCH		
APRIL		
MAY		
JUNE		
JULY		
AUGUST		
SEPTEMBER		
OCTOBER		
NOVEMBER		
DECEMBER		

If you make about six huge expansions and contractions *several times a day*, you will double your expansion in about a year to 18 months! That may mean no more worrying about long phrases. You should keep this up until your expansion/contraction is around four to five inches (10 – 12.5 cms). It is not the size or your body that counts, though big people do have some advantage; it's the amount by which you *expand and contract* that counts. Even small, thin people can obtain a large difference. It's all a question of

_______________, _______________ and _______________ _______________!

Finally, check yourself against a long musical phrase you know well and see whether each week you can last out for a longer time before you have to stop due to lack of breath. Mark your stopping place each day.

About twelve to eighteen months of these exercises should double your expansion, possibly even sooner. You will certainly notice the difference in your performances.

Some more advice about the relationship between the air supply and your tone can be found in Practice Book 6.

BREATHING AND MUSICAL PHRASING

Find a sentence containing commas and semicolons. There are plenty in this book. Notice what they do to a sentence. Notice where you take a breath.

1 They contribute to the *sense* of the sentence
2 They assist in the *forward flow* of the meaning.
3 Your breathing can be part of the way you express the meaning of the writer.

So it is in music.

Breathing marks are not enemies. Yes, they are necessary but they should become part of the expression of music and not a human failing. Prick yourself with a pin. Before you howl in anguish, you breathe in quickly. Think about this. The quickly indrawn breath becomes *part* of your expression of pain. So it is in music.

Breathing in music can't really be explained; the most we can do is provide guidelines. *Breathing, and breathing places, can only be proved by the performance.* There are many opinions on where to breathe. Breathing can *add* to the expression of a musical phrase. *It can also detract from it.*

Consider this phrase from the opening of Fauré's Fantasie:-

FANTASIE

FAURÉ

There are many possibilities for breathing. In bar 2, the bass line is rising and continues to rise into bar 3. This indicates a forward musical movement. It's not *bad* to breathe at (A), simply undesirable. *But*, supposing a slight crescendo is made during bar 2 and continued *right up to* the breath at (A), if then the second note of bar 3 is played *as if the crescendo continues*, then the breath is not only unnoticed, but contributes to the forward motion of the music. If the performer were to make a *diminuendo* to bar three and take the breath at (A), it would halt the forward motion of the phrase. This is what often happens. Breathing, then, can contribute a great deal toward the sense and forward motion of a musical phrase. If a deliberate diminuendo, or announcement, is made that a breath is to be taken, it then interrupts the forward motion.

Back to Fauré. Marked below are a variety of options on where to breathe. They all depend on where you consider the phrase-bits end, or temporarily rest. As mentioned before, breath (A) isn't really good because of the ascending bass line. (B) is not satisfactory as the phrase continues through the bar to the D sharp – E resolution. (C) is good if the natural diminuendo (suspension-resolution of D sharp to E) is continued through the breath into bar five. (D) is the parallel place to (A) and is not good for the same reason. (E) is parallel to (B); there is no natural end to the phrase here. (F) is parallel to (C) and should, logically, be taken. However, because of the natural direction of notes in bar eight, many would prefer the breath at (G). (H) and (I) both sound daft, although if (A) is taken, then perhaps (H) and (I) should be as well. (J) could be taken, though it would interrupt the rising melody. (K) is parallel to (G), (L) is parallel to (A).

The F sharp in bar thirteen has a natural forward motion through bar fourteen on to the surprise F natural at bar fifteen. Therefore (M) isn't good and (N) would ruin the natural phrase-end at (O). (P) is, of course, parallel to (O).

How many other breaths can you find and justify?

The study of this passage leads to a conclusion; although *where* to breathe is important, it is also *how* the breath is taken; *how* it is prepared; *how* the interruption is restarted after the breath.

BREATHING WILL PRESENT FEW PROBLEMS WHEN IT BECOMES VERY IMPORTANT TO YOU TO CONTINUE THE FORWARD FLOW OF THE MUSICAL PHRASE.

Here are some guidelines:—

1) Mark your breathing in where you think it should be in a piece you are playing at the moment. Ask yourself, as a guide:—
   (a) what is the harmony doing?
   (b) what is the bass doing?
   (c) where is the melody going?

2) Don't divide the music up into bite-sized chunks in order to make it look evenly spaced. You can take more than one breath in a bar if you wish, or if you *have* to. Several short breaths can result in a long following phrase which may be more musically satisfying.

3) Practise how to breathe quickly. See below for some exercises.

4) *Use your breathing places to make the music more expressive: breathing then becomes part of your way of expressing the music.*

5) When marking your breathing, look both ahead and behind to the parallel phrases which, as nearly as possible, should correspond; but consider points (1) (a), (b) and (c) above.

6) The note before a breath must not diminuendo or be musically terminated (⟩) as this announces the breath long before it happens. You wouldn't put in the diminuendo (or Note Ending – see P.B. No. 1) if you were *not* going to breathe.

7) The note before a breath must remain *beautiful* until the breath takes place.

8) The note immediately after a breath must take over where the previous note left off. Much more clever still would be to assume that the crescendo *continues* through the breath and therefore the note after takes over at the crescendo point it *would* have reached had the breath not taken place!

9) The note after a breath must be *more* musical and expressive than the one before the breath.

Here are two exercises to work at:—

1) With your flute, first practise taking a breath in quickly, completely filling the lungs. Do you make a noise when taking in air? If you do this could be caused by:-
   (a) raised shoulders, therefore, a tight throat.
   (b) not opening your mouth wide enough; drop your jaw and with your teeth together, suck in air. It should feel cold on your teeth. Repeat with your teeth further apart; this time the cold air affects the back of your throat. Open your mouth and throat so that the cold feeling is well down in your lungs. Your breathing will also be silent.
   (c) your head is lowered with your chin near your chest. Hold your head up!
   (d) perhaps, just a tight throat.

Test yourself with a piece well-known to you and check the points above.

2) Play the first long note below; *as quickly as possible*, stop, take a breath, and restart your note. Work at shortening the time taken to breathe. You will quickly find that the time taken and the amount of air taken in are directly connected to your ability to open the throat and mouth wide enough.

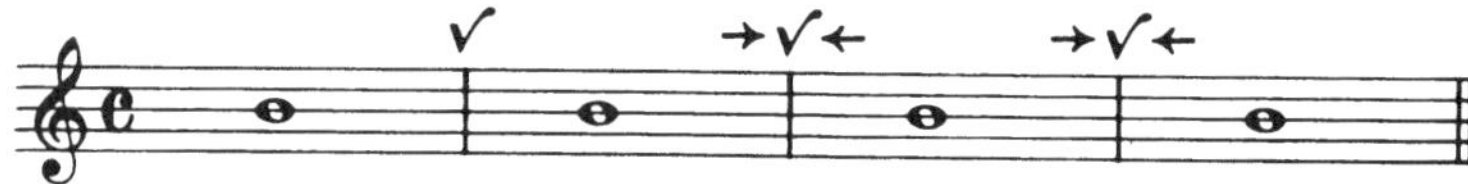

EXPRESSIVE SCALES AND ARPEGGIOS

These are amongst the most important exercises for experiencing the movement of a beautiful tone through the compass of the flute. Mould your tone to the key you are in. Push the intensity of your tone forward as you ascend; learn to return to your starting point when descending; let each phrase of two bars lead naturally to the next pair. Use your tone to change key (see Practice Book 1, TONE – page 24). These exercises are useful both to study the movement of expression and as daily warm-up exercises.

EXPRESSIVE SCALES

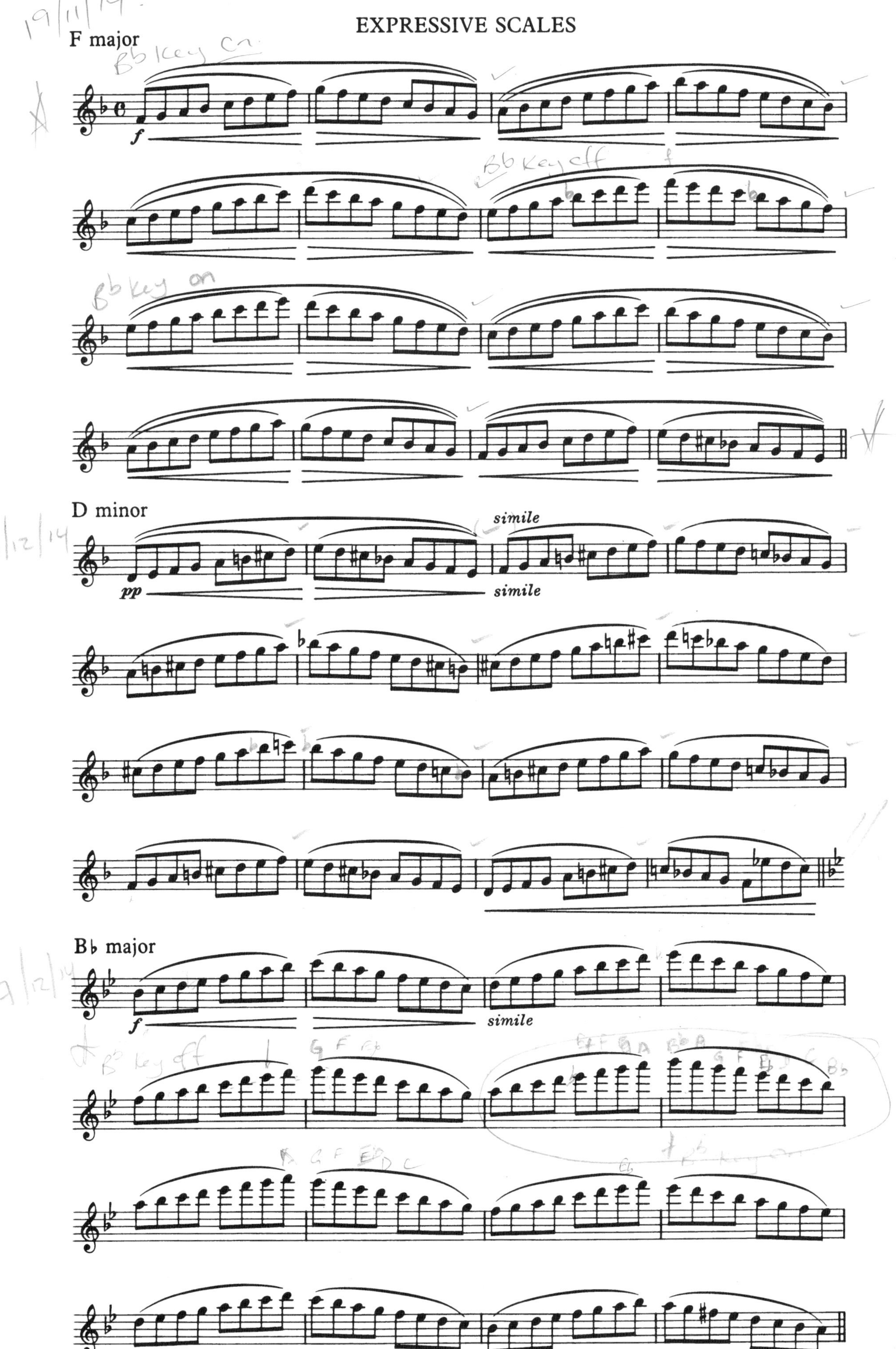

G minor
pp
simile
simile
E♭ major
f
simile
C minor
pp
simile

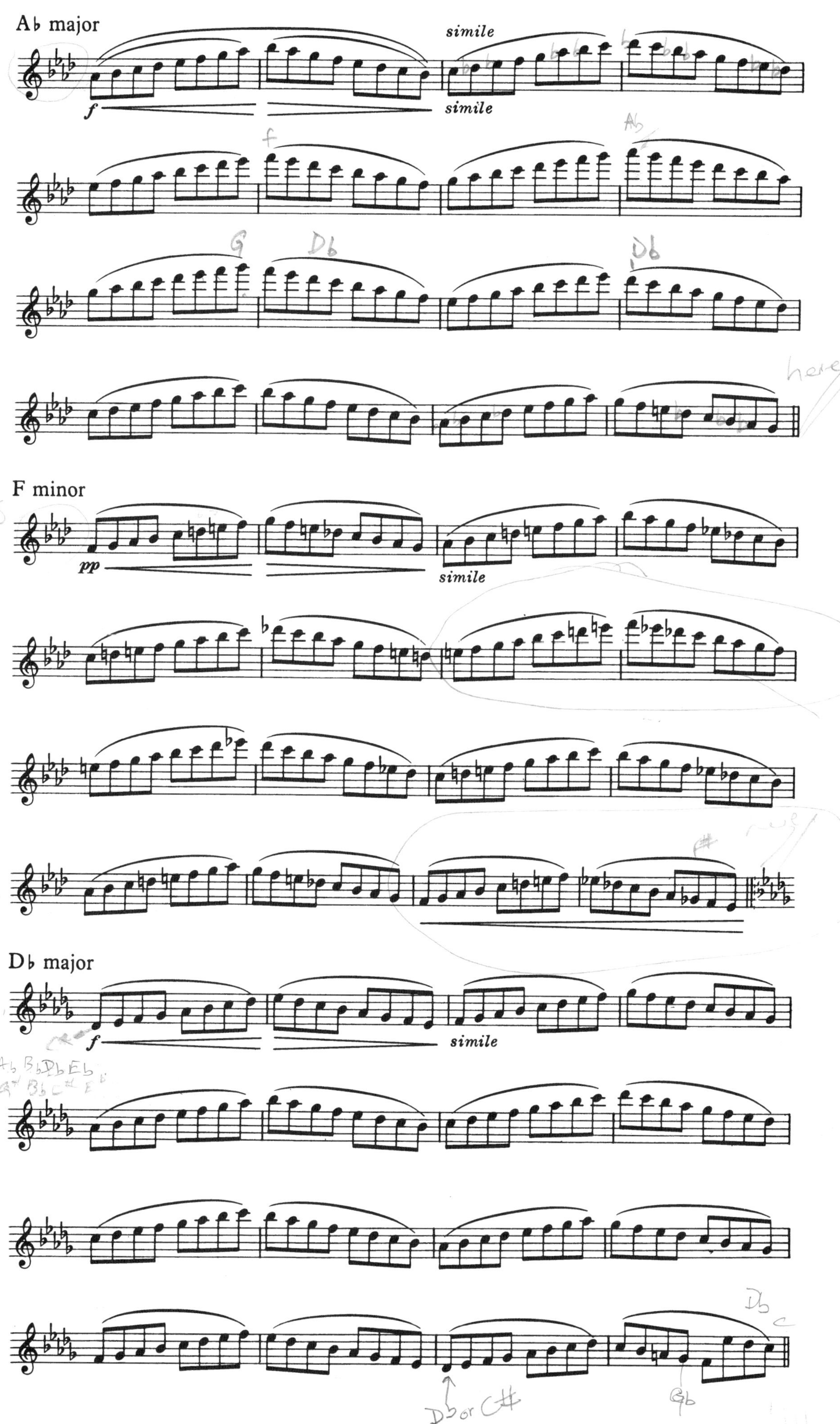
A♭ major
simile
f
simile
F minor
pp
simile
D♭ major
f
simile

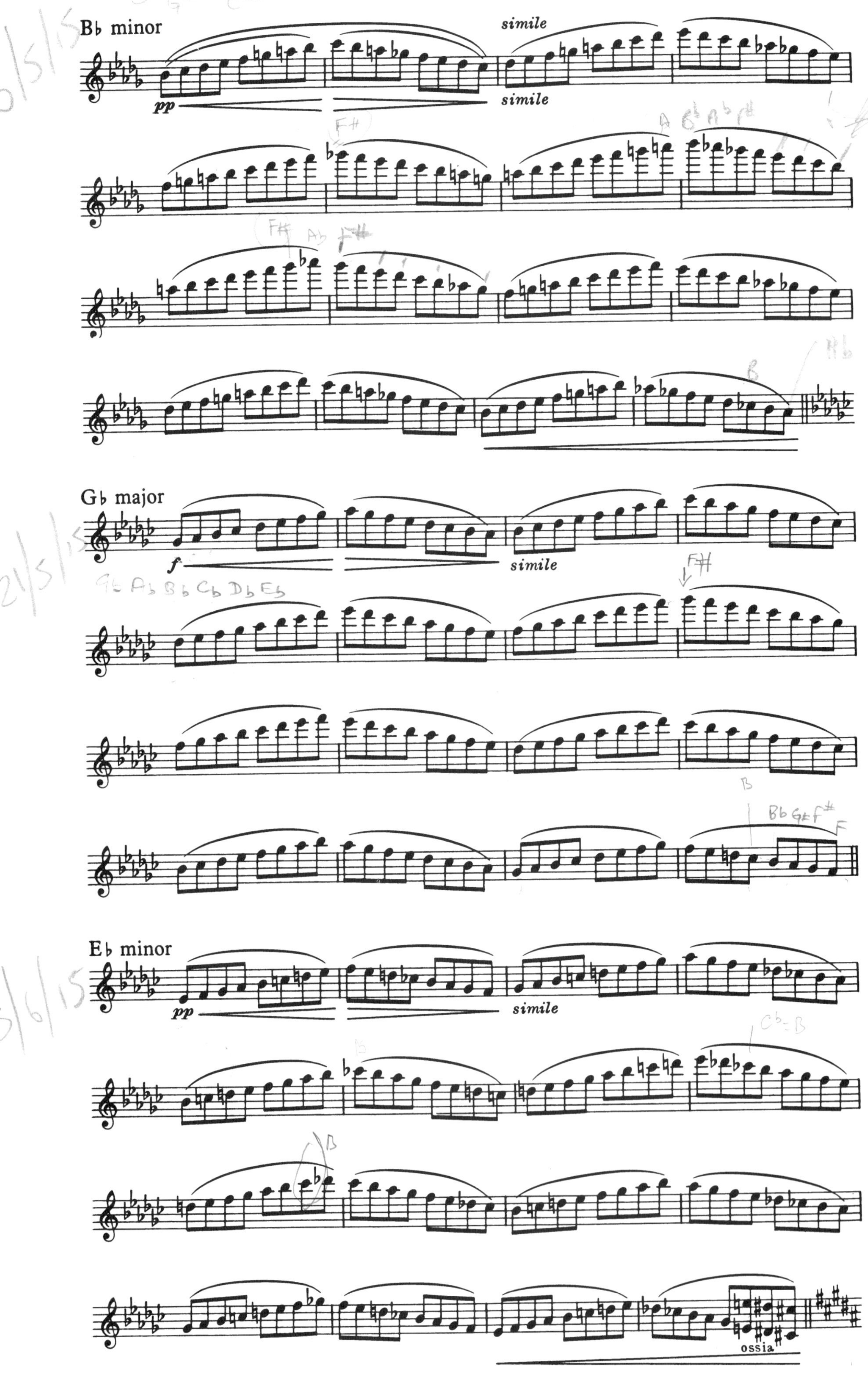
Bb minor
simile
pp
simile
Gb major
f
simile
Eb minor
pp
simile
ossia

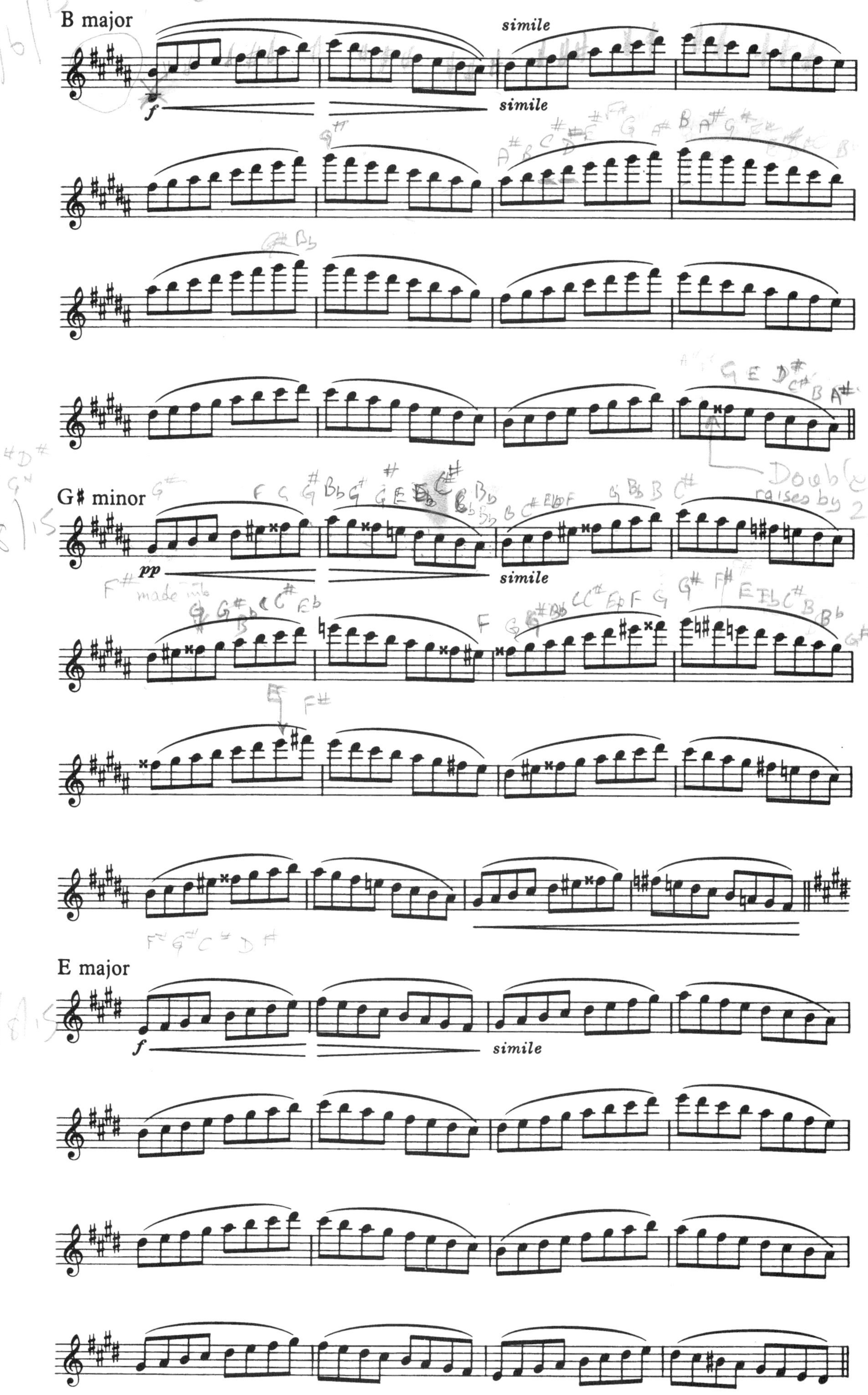
B major
simile
f
simile
G♯ minor
pp
simile
E major
f
simile

C♯ minor

simile

pp *simile*

A major

f *simile*

F♯ minor

pp *simile*

D major

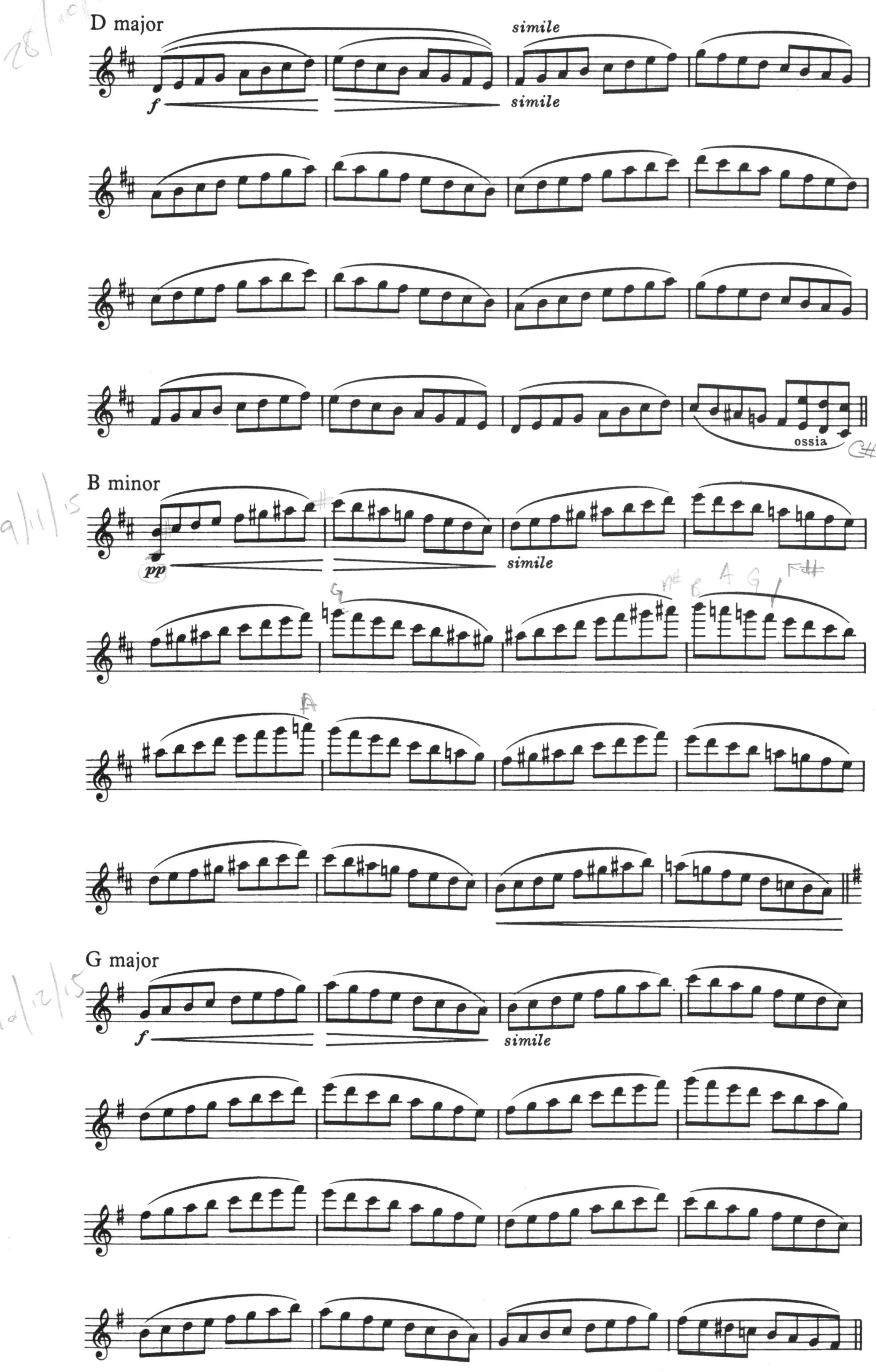

E minor
simile
pp
simile
C major
f
simile
A minor
pp
simile
f

EXPRESSIVE ARPEGGIOS

Practise as in the Expressive Scales.

Learn to make your tone SING.

Feel happy! The weather may be lousy; pretend it isn't.

If you are not enjoying them with the resultant improvement in your tone, you are sick: put your flute in its case and go to bed.

(BUT PRACTISE TWICE TOMORROW!)

PRACTISE THIS ARPEGGIO SECTION IN TWO WAYS:–

Remember Practice Book 3 ARTICULATION, page 9 exercise 6? LOOK IT UP. In 18th century music the slur = diminuendo; don't shorten the second note.

EXPRESSIVE ARPEGGIOS

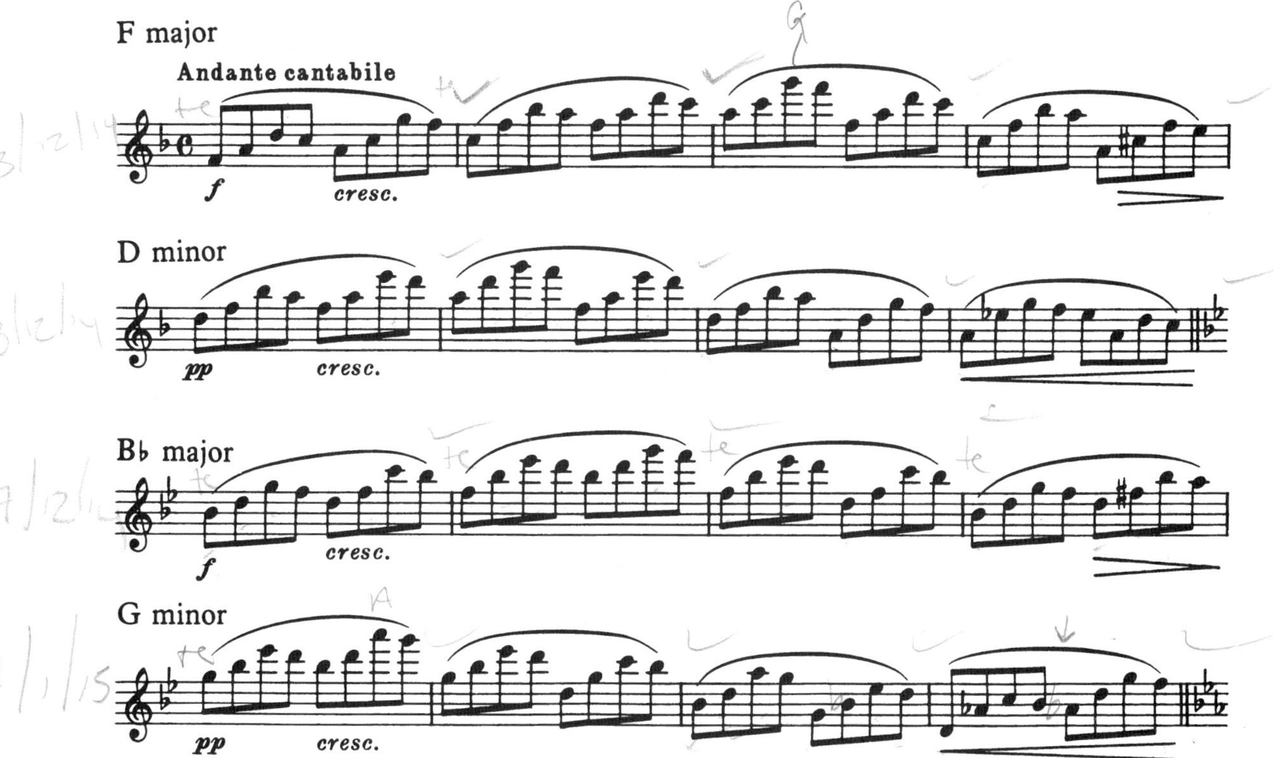

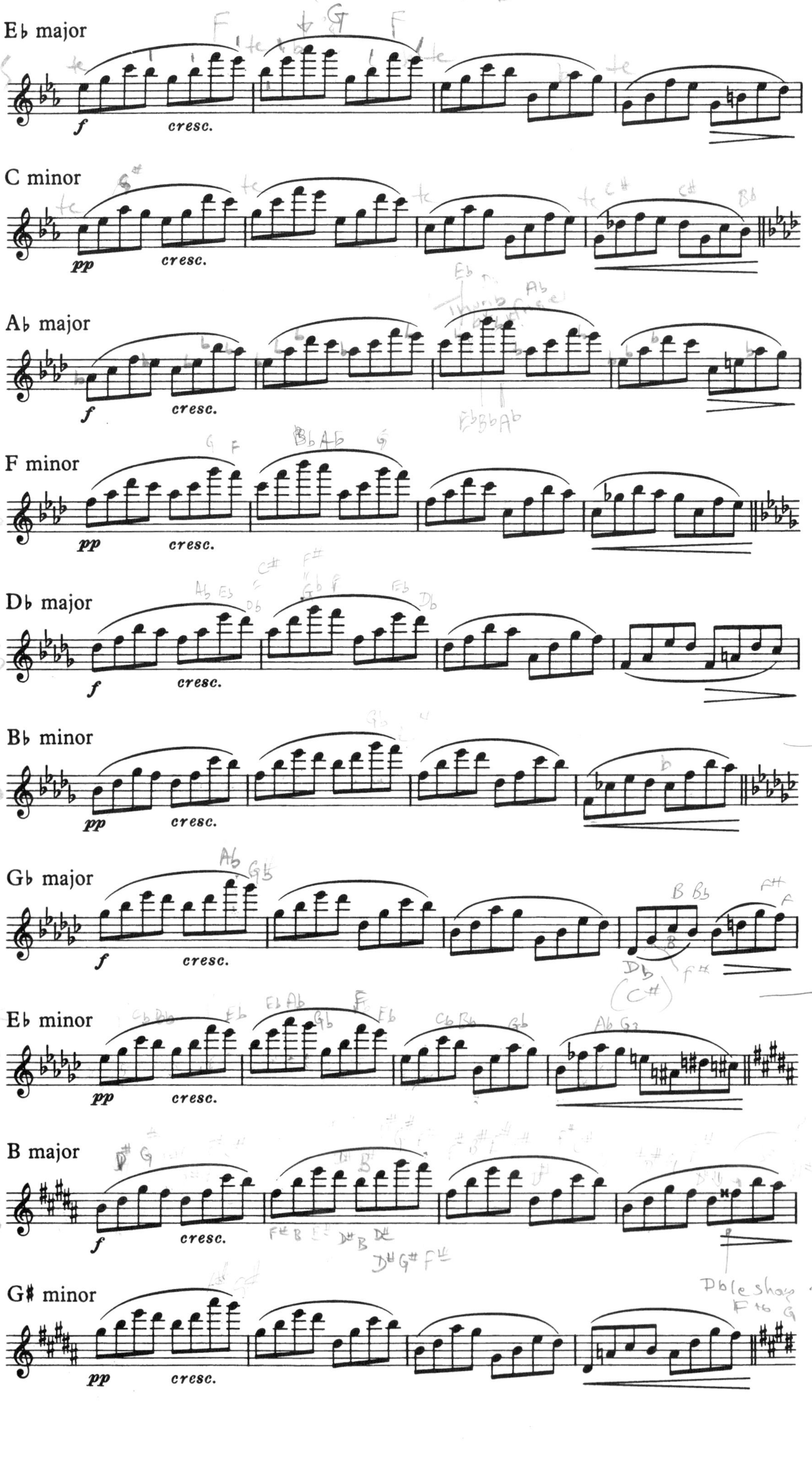

Eb major

f *cresc.*

C minor

pp *cresc.*

Ab major

f *cresc.*

F minor

pp *cresc.*

Db major

f *cresc.*

Bb minor

pp *cresc.*

Gb major

f *cresc.*

Eb minor

pp *cresc.*

B major

f *cresc.*

G# minor

pp *cresc.*

E major
f
cresc.
C♯ minor
pp
cresc.
A major
f
cresc.
F♯ minor
pp
cresc.
D major
f
cresc.
B minor
pp
cresc.
G major
f
cresc.
E minor
pp
cresc.
C major
f
cresc.
A minor
pp
cresc.

TECHNICAL SCALES AND ARPEGGIOS
SECTIONS ONE, TWO AND THREE

All the technical exercises in Practice Book 2 – TECHNIQUE – were designed as basic practice material for this next section.

It really is impossible to develop a good technique and to be able to exercise control over your fingers, lips and tongue without scales and arpeggios.

Here are some hints on how to tackle this section:—

(a) Play them through at any convenient speed. If they are really beyond your technical capabilities at this stage then work at Practice Book 2 thoroughly first, especially the third octave.

(b) Always play scales and arpeggios with your *best* tone.

(c) Always play them with the same expressiveness that you used in the previous section; they must sound beautiful.

(d) If the third octave presents any problems, mark the section as a group of twelve notes (to cover all the offending notes) and practise these later for a short time. Every third day, leave the scales and arpeggios and concentrate only on these groups of twelve notes. In this way, they will rapidly improve and will soon equal the lower two octaves.

(e) Mark the keys you find most difficult and practise *only* these every third day.

(f) Read, once again, the Preface to this, and every other Practice Book. Yes, I know you've read it before, but read it again. *This means you!*

SECTION ONE – SCALES: CHROMATIC, WHOLE TONE, MAJOR AND MINOR

MAJOR AND MINOR SCALES

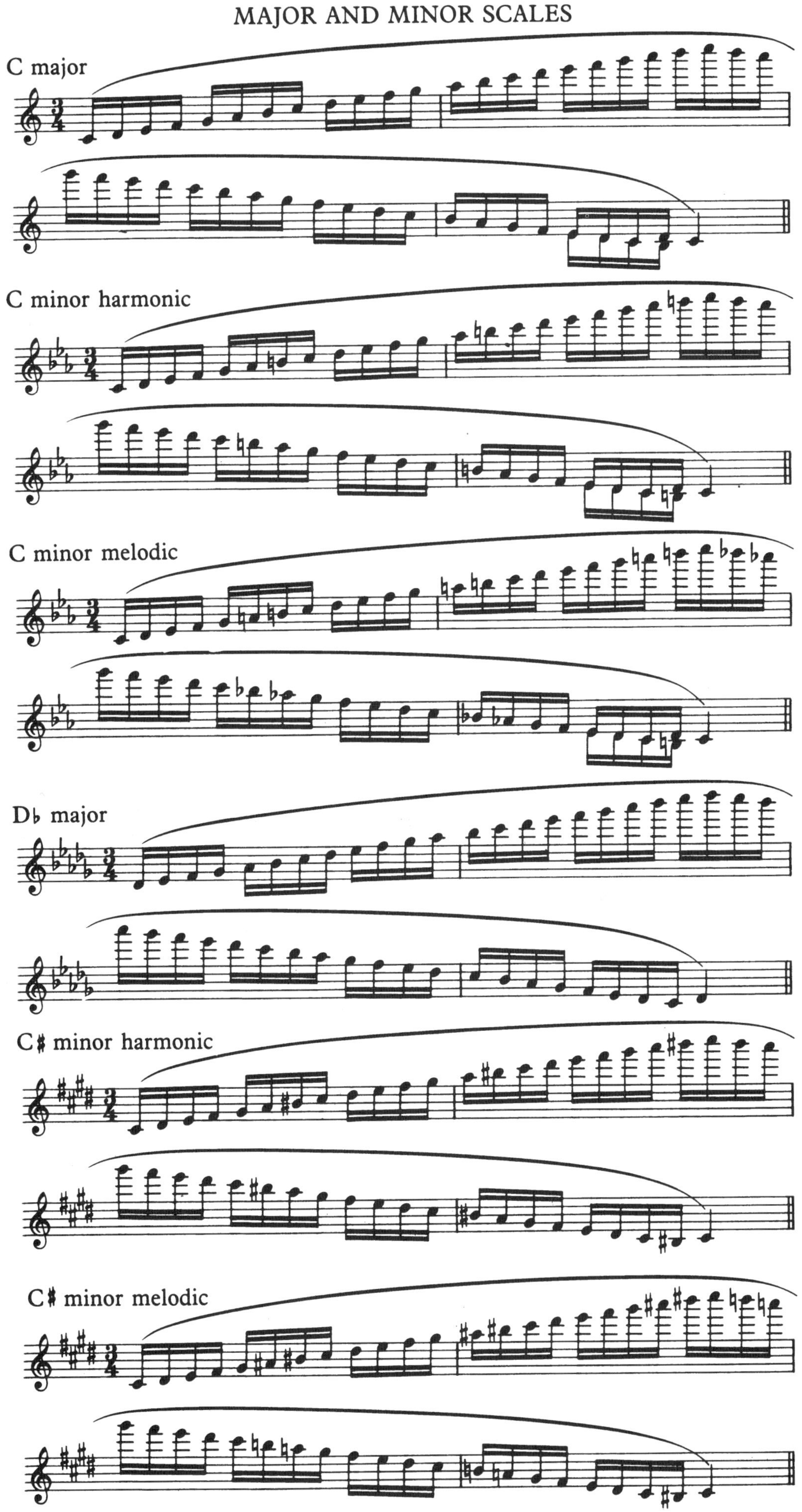

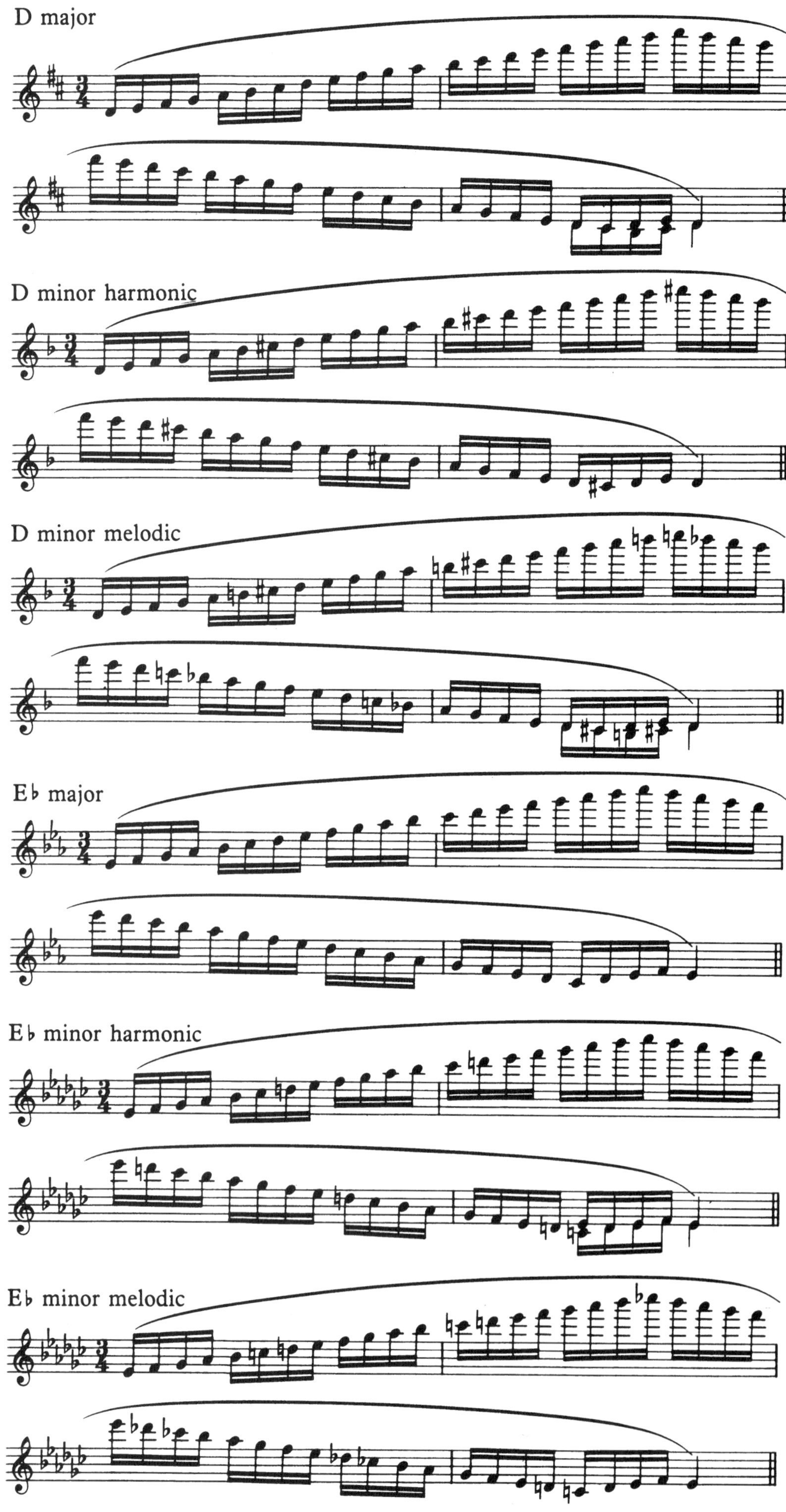
D major
D minor harmonic
D minor melodic
E♭ major
E♭ minor harmonic
E♭ minor melodic

E major
E minor harmonic
E minor melodic
F major
F minor harmonic
F minor melodic

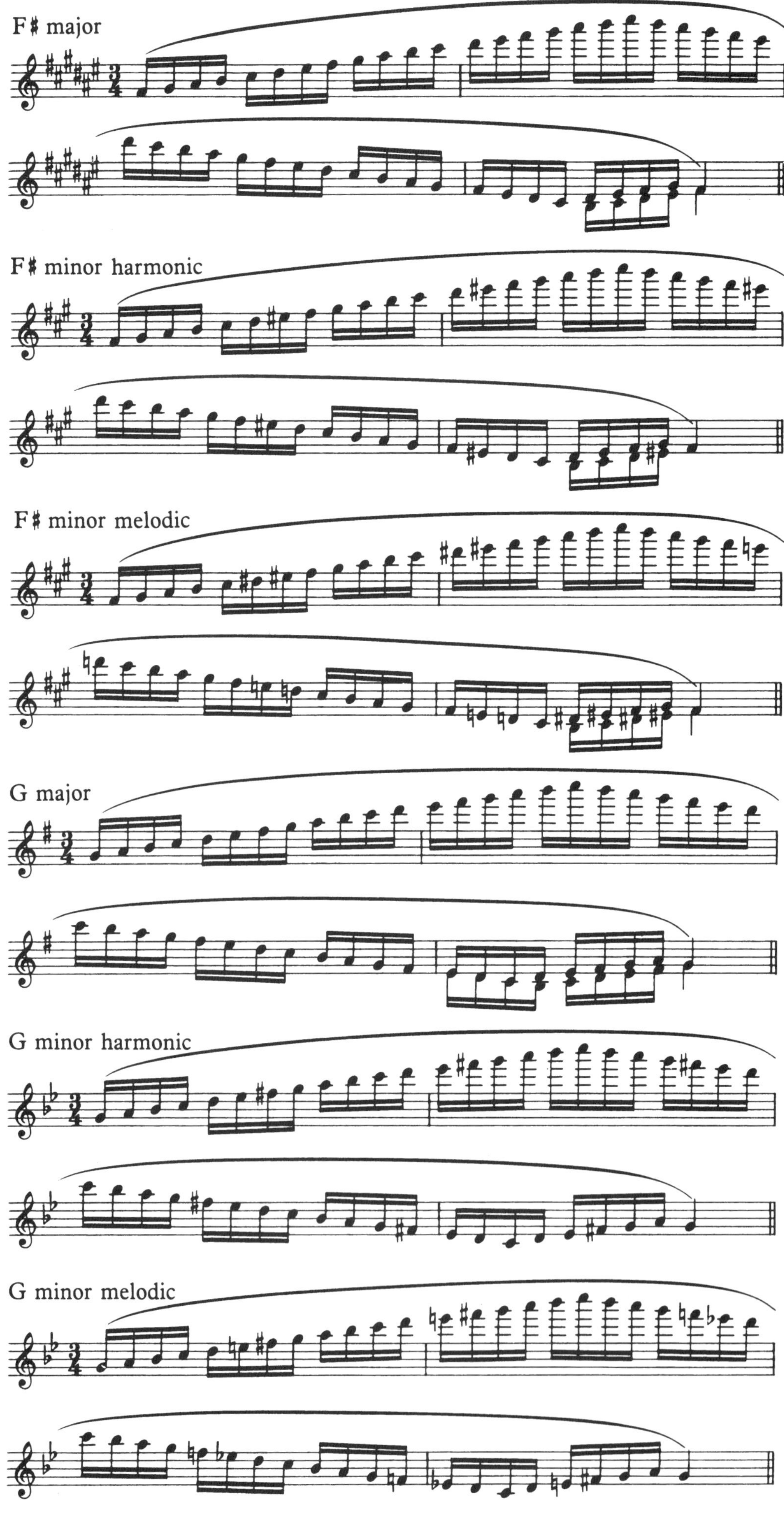
F♯ major
F♯ minor harmonic
F♯ minor melodic
G major
G minor harmonic
G minor melodic

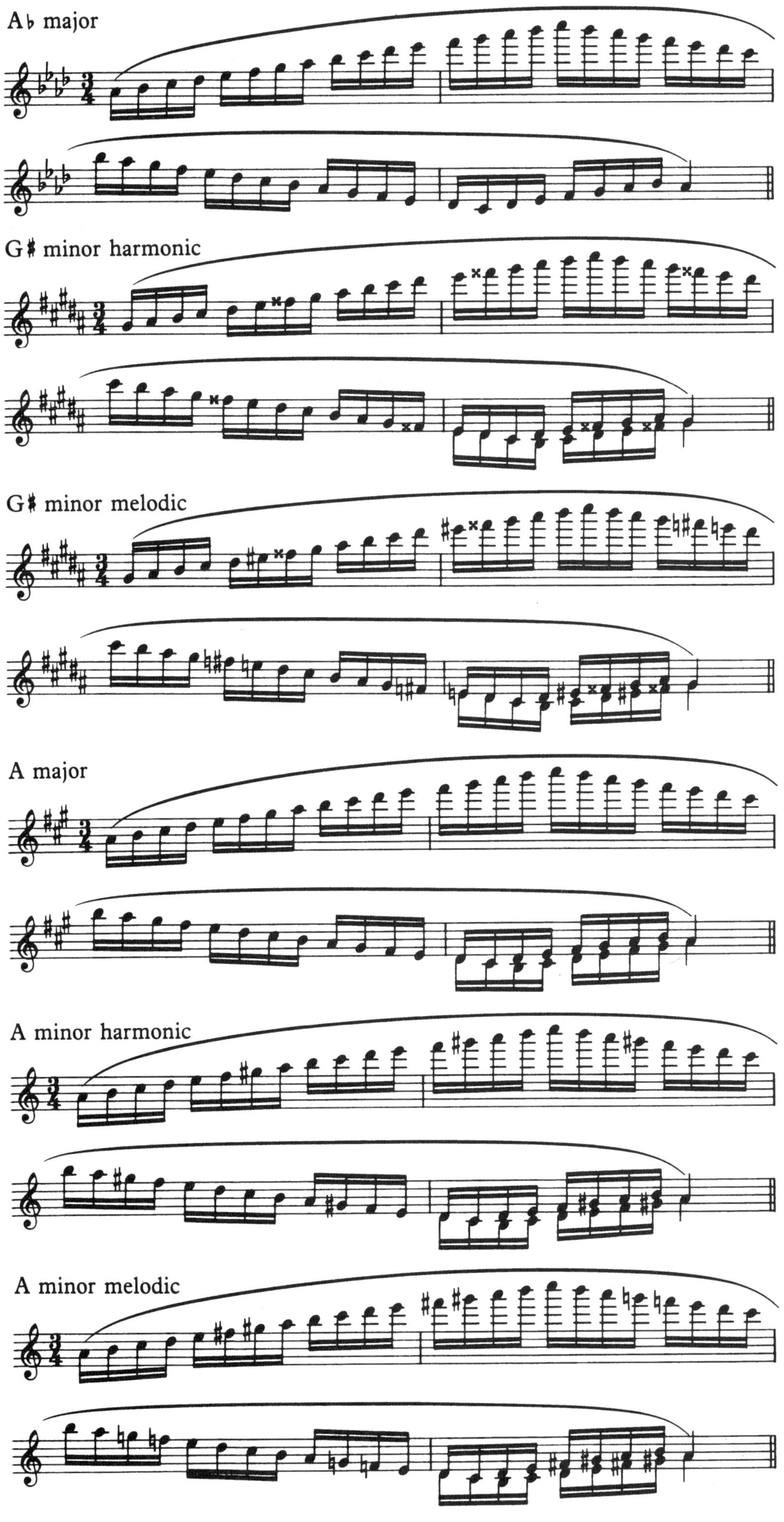
A♭ major
G♯ minor harmonic
G♯ minor melodic
A major
A minor harmonic
A minor melodic

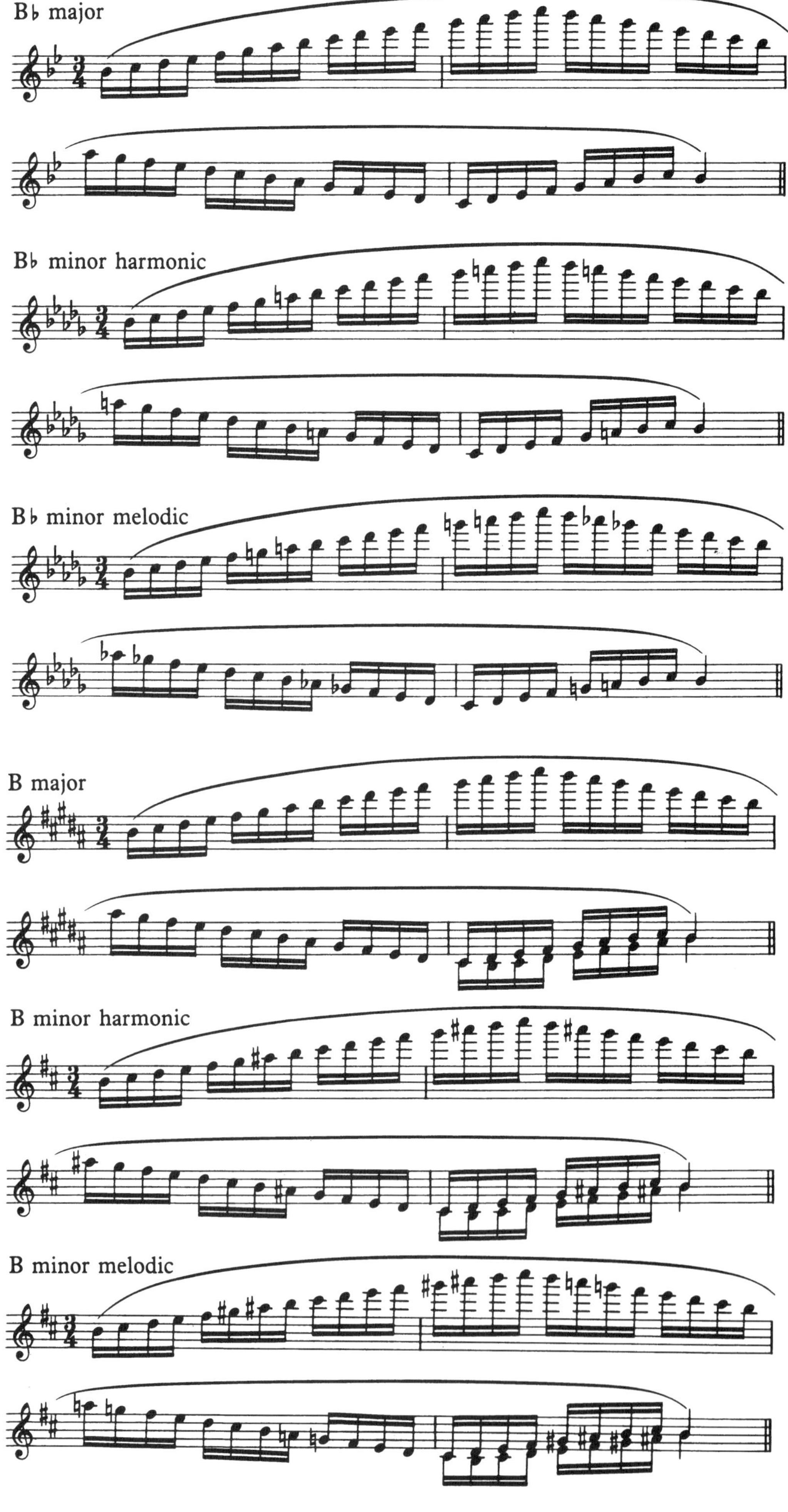
B♭ major
B♭ minor harmonic
B♭ minor melodic
B major
B minor harmonic
B minor melodic

SECTION TWO – ARPEGGIOS: MAJOR, MINOR AND DIMINISHED

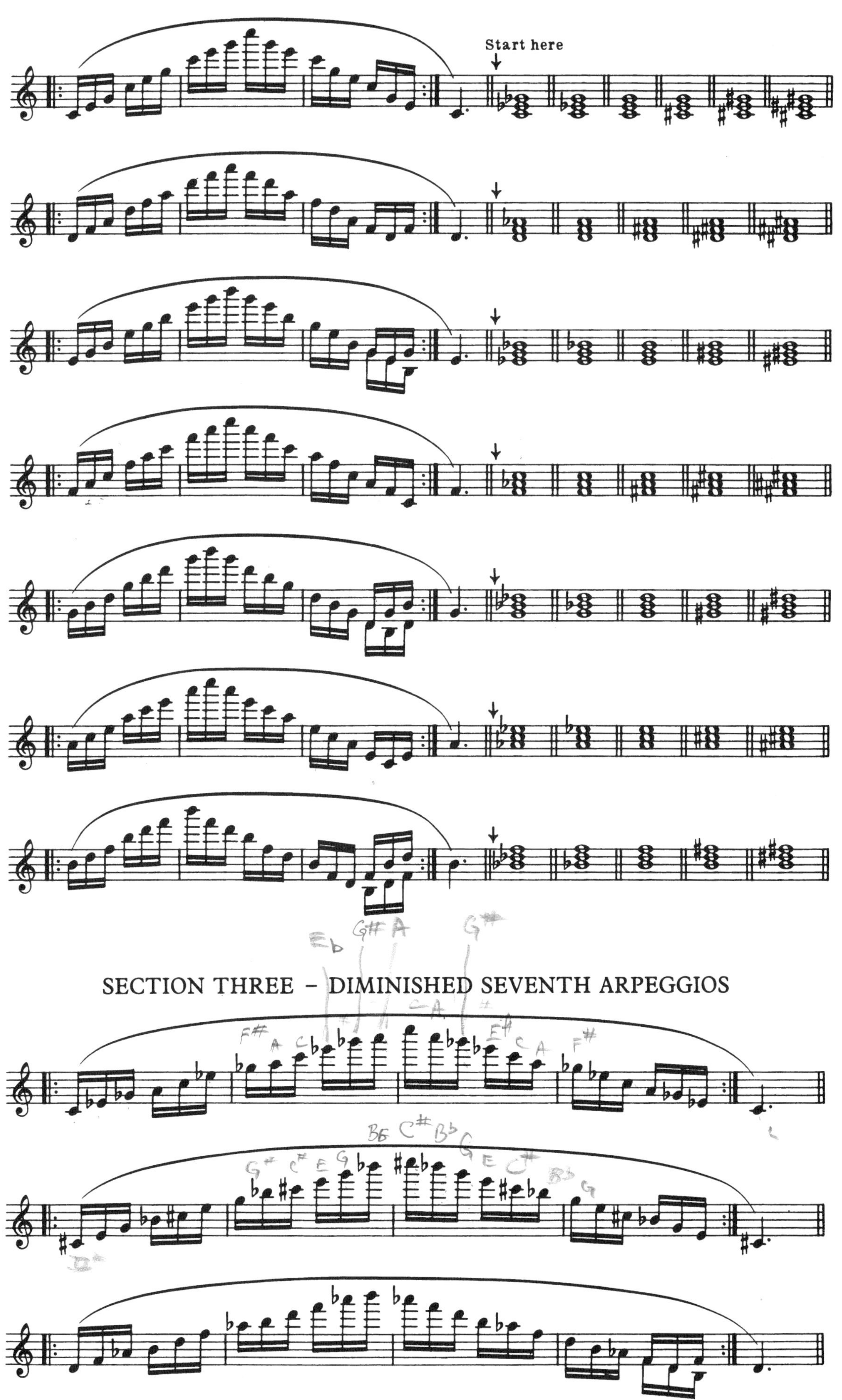

SECTION THREE – DIMINISHED SEVENTH ARPEGGIOS

OTHER ARPEGGIOS OF THE SEVENTH

SECTIONS FOUR, FIVE AND SIX

SCALES IN THIRDS AND BROKEN ARPEGGIOS

These represent the final stage in the acquisition of a basic technique. If you have got so far, nothing must stop you from finishing the job off properly.

By exercising your fingers on these, and the previous scales, you have taught them note patterns which occur in most of the flute literature most of the time. Expressed another way, you have learned 95% of 90% of the entire flute repertoire! Or, you have learned 85.5% of all flute music.
It's time well spent.
So, get to it!

SECTION FOUR – MAJOR SCALES IN THIRDS

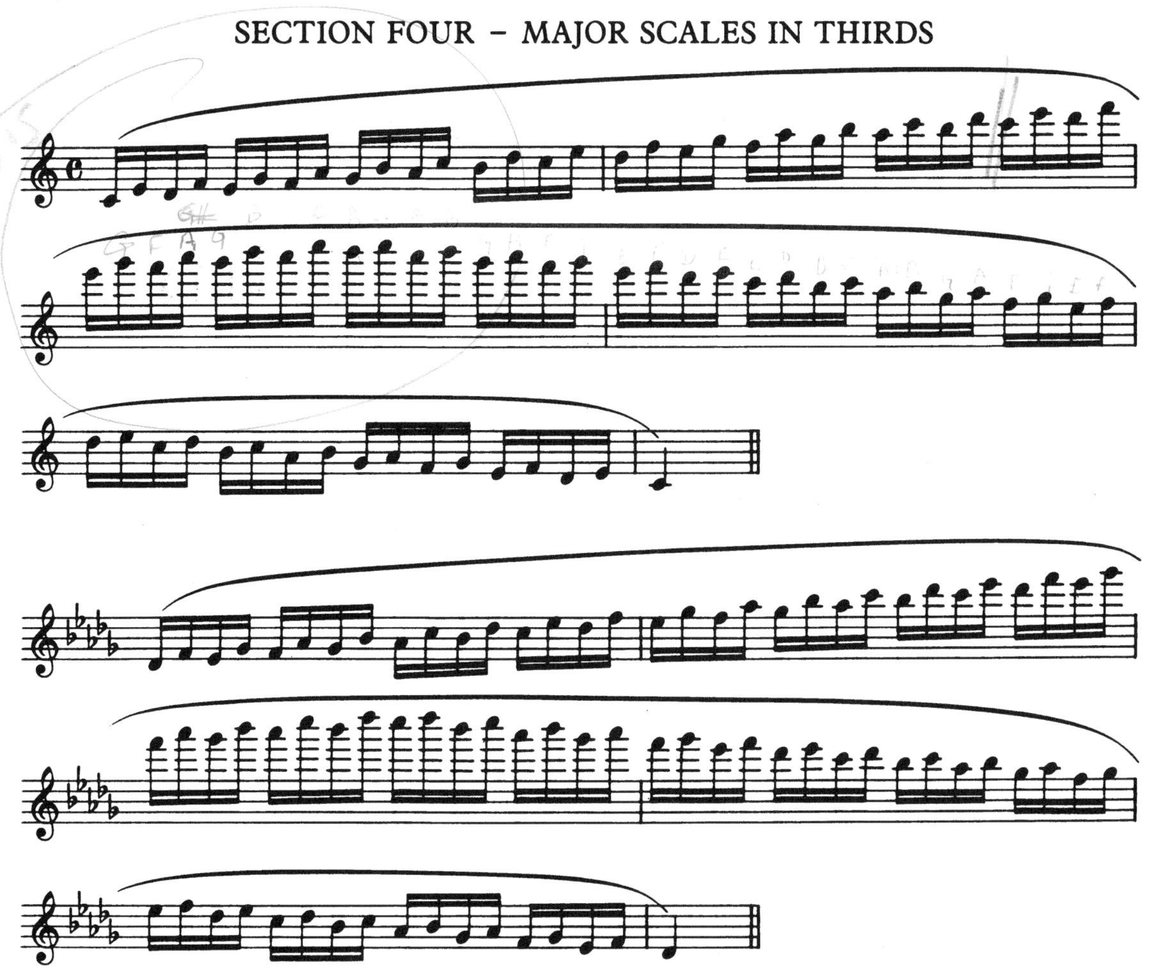

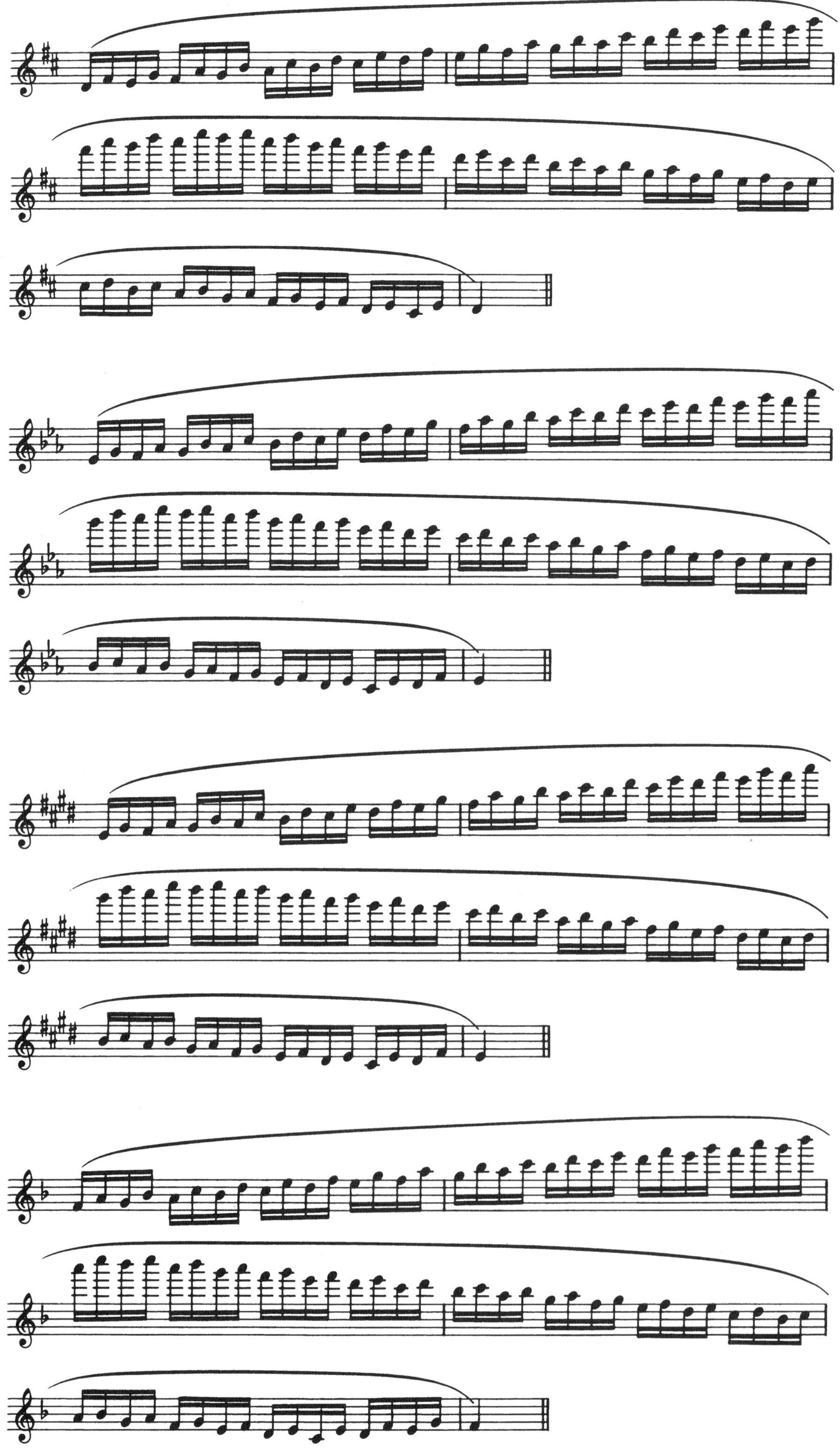

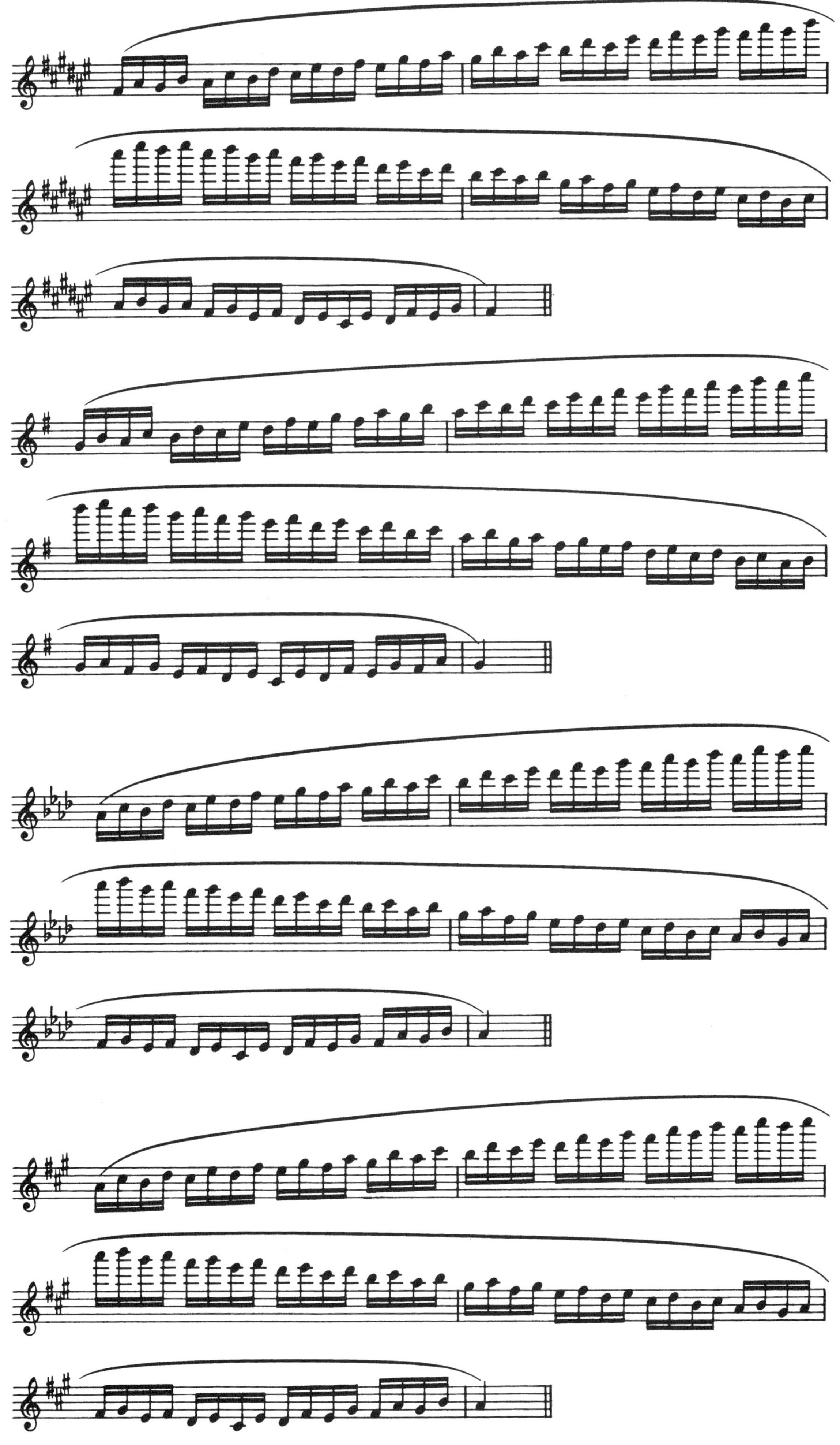

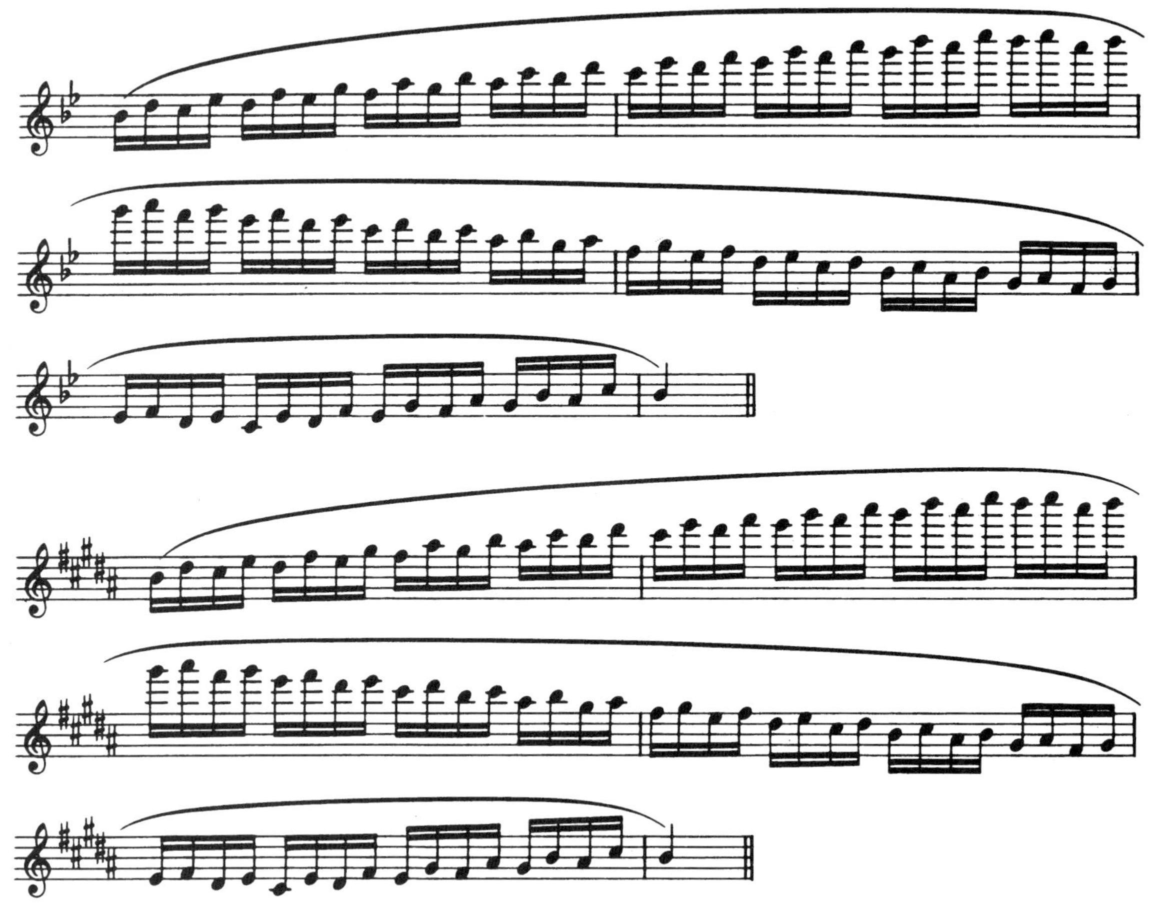

MINOR SCALES IN THIRDS

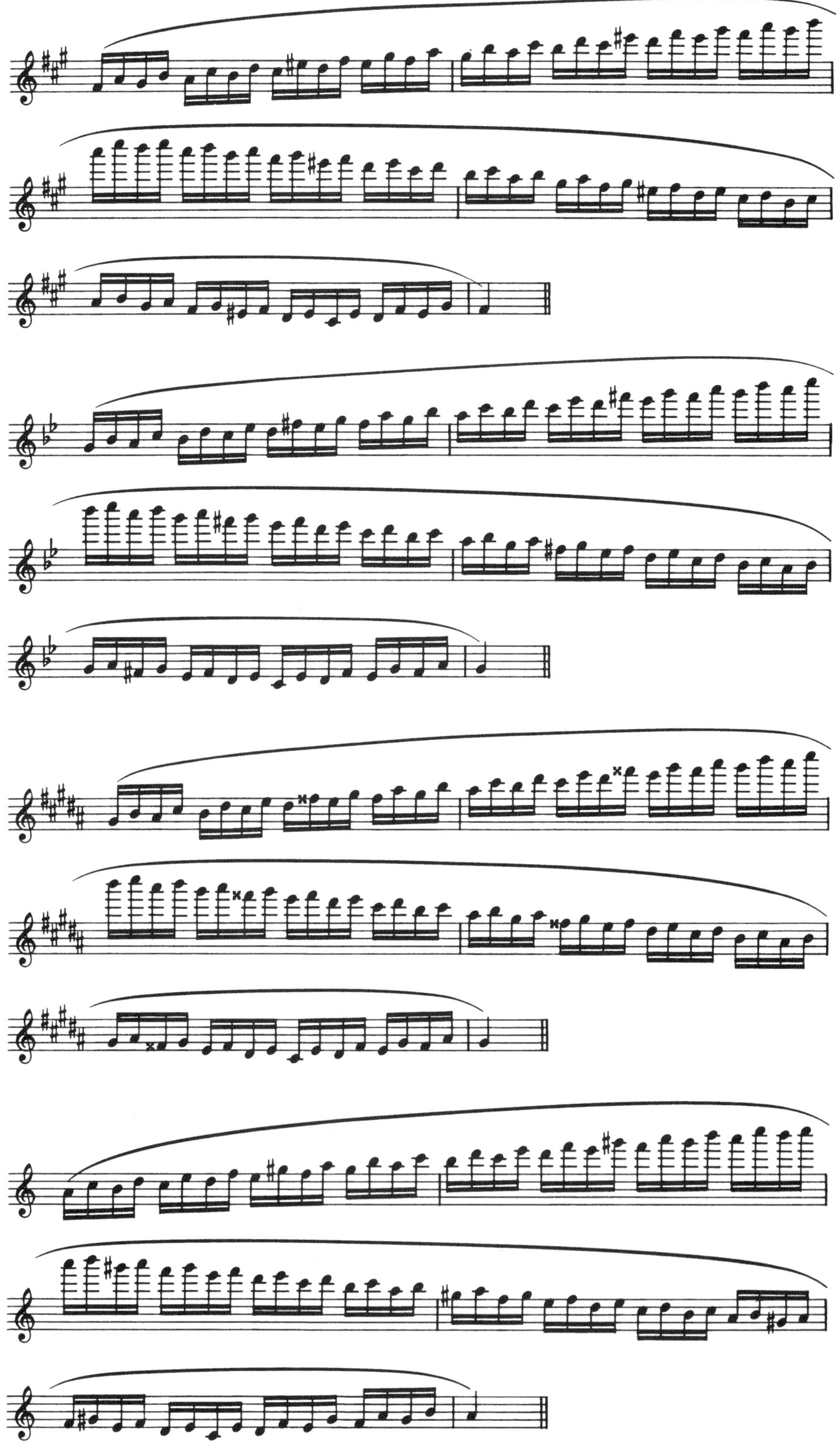

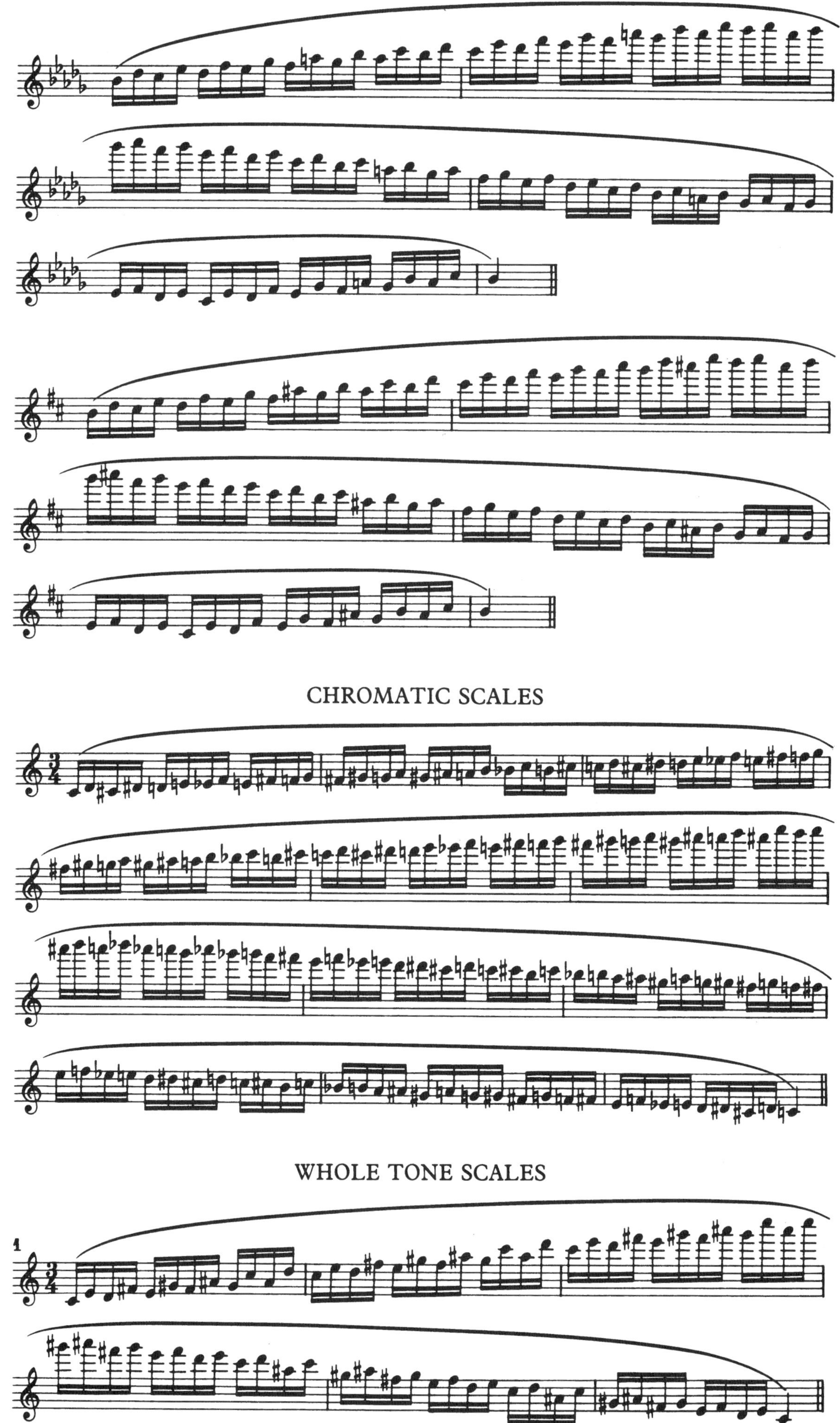
CHROMATIC SCALES
WHOLE TONE SCALES
1

SECTION FIVE – DIMINISHED ARPEGGIOS

SECTION FIVE – BROKEN ARPEGGIOS

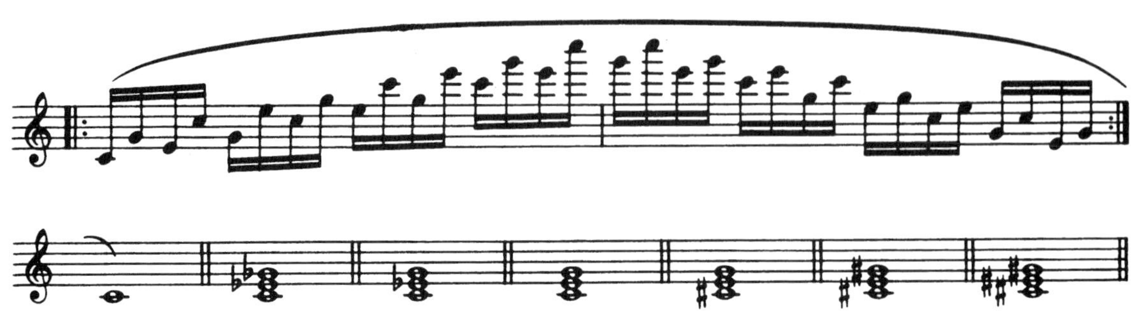

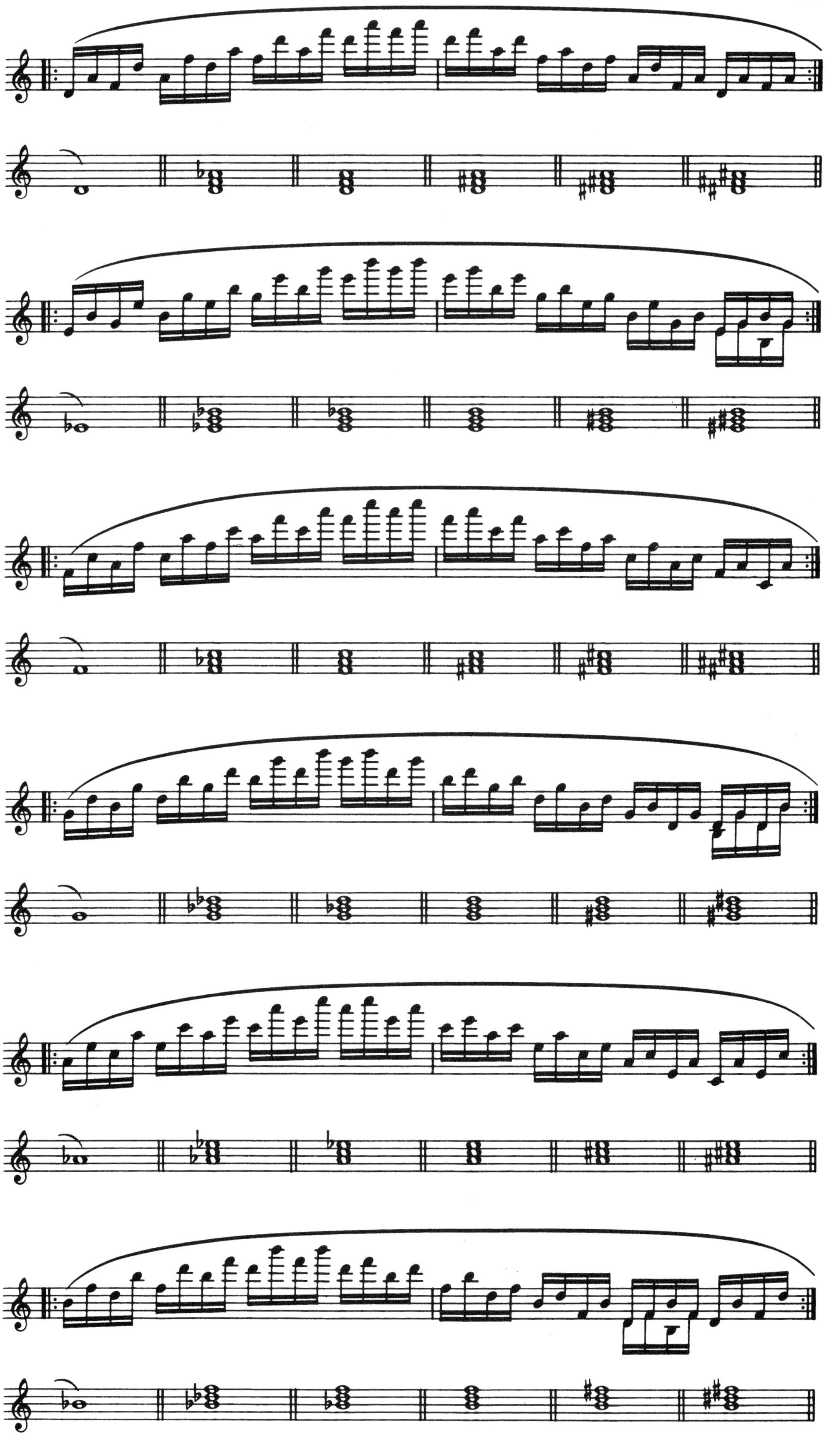

SECTION SIX – BROKEN ARPEGGIOS ON THE SEVENTH

IMPROVISATION

Improvisation is the art of instantaneous musical invention, and generally means playing melodic patterns or melodies from a given series of chords, or from a bass line.

Improvisation is like talking without a script but talking about a *particular* subject.

Do you need a script when holding a conversation with someone? Of course not. You also don't need printed music to be able to make musical sounds. But to make sense of your musical sounds, you do need a subject on which to improvise.

The two most common forms of improvisation are jazz and baroque, or 18th century improvisation. Surprisingly, the two are very similar, as they are both based on the same chord progressions. It's the style which is different. This section will be concerned only with improvisation in the baroque and classical styles.

The studies are in approximate order of difficulty and start with simple exercises for chord and cadence recognition. Ideally, the keyboard part should be played to a group of performers (on any instruments) and repeated, without stopping, over and over again, each player having his turn at improvising. In this way, ideas are fed from one player to another.

Begin by freeing your mind from the printed page by playing as many 'variations' as you can on the three C's. Five examples are given. Try about twenty or thirty.

Before trying example (b), have you exhausted every possibility in your imagination? Different rhythms? Passing notes?

Examples: –

Examples: –

Exercise (c) gives a bass: put a cadence to it. Make several different cadences, some simple, some elaborate. Melodic examples are given which fit this bass.

Example (d) is a little longer and leads us on to the next stage.

(1) and (2) are examples of phrases from the flute repertoire. Study them. Either ask someone to play the basses repeatedly whilst you improvise to them, or, tape-record the bass repeatedly, and play to your own recording. Above the bass is what the composer originally wrote.

NOW, ON TO IMPROVISATION

There are some rules: –
In the beginning,

1 play anything that comes into your head. As you become bolder try to get a 'feel' for the harmonic movement of the bass line.
2 relax; there are no 'right' or 'wrong' notes; just notes in good or bad taste.
3 Quantz said – 'My advice is not to give yourself over too much to variations, but rather to apply yourself to playing a plain air nobly, truly, and clearly'. Don't therefore, go crazy and try to fit in as many notes as possible; rather, be economical and simple.

The basses are taken from the works of Telemann, Couperin, Vivaldi, Rameau, Handel and others. Chords have been added in the right hand part to make it easier to hear the harmonic progression of the bass. A good idea with a group of players is for the pianist to call out the names of the chords as he plays them and for the players to play *any* note of that chord. This quickly helps the players to get the 'feel' of the progressions.

Once the performers have understood the chordal progression, the right hand should be omitted, or just touched upon occasionally to assist with any particular difficulty.

Fit a tune or cadence to this bass. The chords are provided to assist you.

During the next few weeks, choose basses which appeal to you. Don't be too ambitious too soon. Do the easier ones first.

From now on, *don't* look at the right hand chords to help you improvise. Rather, keep the chord progression in your head.

6

7

8

9

10

Avoid following the direction of the bass line in your melody: contrary motion sounds best.

11

12
13
14
15

16

The sequences on page 33 of Volume 2 – TECHNIQUE should now be practised from memory, as should the Expressive Scales and Arpeggios in this book.

17

18

19

20

21
22
23
24

25
26
27
28
Slow

29
30
1
2
D.C.
31
FINE
D.C.

32
33
34
35

WHAT NOW?

You have, for sure, by now, a greater understanding of chordal progressions in 18th century music to the point where you are instantaneously *composing* music. Good eh?

Take some slow movements of Handel or Telemann sonatas. With your accompanist, improvise upon the melody either by changing it, as an exercise, or embellishing and decorating it. You must acquire 'good taste'. Read 'The Interpretation of Music' by Thurston Dart as a general introduction. Study Telemann's embellishments to his own slow movements in the 12 Methodische Sonaten, Op. XIII (Bärenreiter). These are very interesting.
Thereafter, the works of J. J. Quantz, C. P. E. Bach and the more recent works of Robert Donington will provide further study in greater depth.

PLAYING FROM MEMORY

All solo pianists and string players play from memory. Wind players sometimes do, but as there is no tradition of memorising concertos, they generally don't. This is a pity as musicians who do play from memory will confirm that it does ultimately lead to a greater freedom of expression in music.

Everyone can play from memory if their approach to it is right. You don't have to spend extra practice time on *acquiring* a 'memory'! *You have already got one.* It just needs exercising. Here are some tips:

1 Don't stare at the music all of the time like a rabbit at a snake. This applies to scales, exercises – in fact anything! Try walking away from the music stand. Look out of the window and continue the piece but don't fret if it goes wrong. You don't need a script to hold a conversation and you don't need music to play the flute.

2 Don't try too hard to be right. If you do slip up, it's hardly likely to start a nuclear war.

   Trying hard to 'get it right' is what stands in the way, most often, of a reliable memory.

   Enjoy the freedom of being without the restraint of a script. This may take time to understand but is well worth the effort.

3 Learn to improvise (see previous section). Learn to 'prelude'. In the 18/19th century, it was common to 'prelude' before playing a study or piece. This entailed playing a sort of cadenza in the same key as the piece but with freedom of rhythm and expression. You don't need to be told what to play: you only need the courage to try it.

4 Read page 33 of Practice Book No. 2. Include these sequences in your daily practice. Gradually learn to play them from memory.

5 Gradually accustom yourself to looking up from your copy whilst playing in public.

NOTE ON THE OMNIBUS EDITION

It is almost twenty years since I wrote the first Practice Book, and nothing has changed very much since 1979, either in the methods of learning or of teaching: tone, technique and articulation exercises are still the foundations of good playing. Only one area (as I predicted then) has changed: players today are more concerned about intonation than they used to be. It still holds true that if a player really wants to acquire a beautiful tone, then the Intonation Studies in Practice Book Four are an indispensable part of that development. This book should be studied in parallel with Practice Book One (Tone).

I have often been asked how I came to write the Practice Books. I was studying with Marcel Moyse at his Master Class in Boswil, Switzerland, an event I attended every summer for twelve years. One morning, in 1967, I was woken up by a student in the next room of our hotel at about 7am. He was practising Moyse's *De la Sonorité* on our shared balcony. He had poor tone. The ends of the notes went flat. The quality of tone was wrong. It was awful. I asked him what he was doing. 'The Tone Exercise from Moyse', he answered, proudly waving the book at me. He seemed to think that possession of the book, and the regular performance of the exercise was all that was needed to acquire a good tone.

That was the moment I decided to write a book on tone which could be easily understood by everyone... But then what about technique, too? It was twelve years before I started writing the first book, and soon they were also published in nine other languages! I hope that they will continue to prove useful to you in the years to come.

Trevor Wye, 1999

Published by
Novello Publishing Limited
14-15 Berners Street, London W1T 3LJ.

Exclusive distributors:
Music Sales Limited
Newmarket Road, Bury St Edmunds,
Suffolk IP33 3YB.

Order No. NOV120851
ISBN 978-0-85360-936-0

Printed in Croatia.

11/07 (64037)